IN CONVERSATION

HENRY MILLER

IN CONVERSATION

---

with Georges Belmont

*Translated from the French by
Antony Macnabb and Harry Scott*

Chicago
Quadrangle Books
1972

FIRST AMERICAN EDITION

First published in France in 1970 by Editions Stock as *Henry Miller—Entretiens de Paris avec Georges Belmont*. Published in England in 1971 by Sidgwick and Jackson Ltd. as *Face to Face with Henry Miller*.

Library of Congress Catalog Card Number: 73-185062
International Standard Book Number: 0-8129-0248-3

IN CONVERSATION

GEORGES BELMONT: I think that the important thing about these conversations we're going to have is – since they are the only ones of any length you have given on French Radio or Television to date – to try and present as complete a picture of you as possible, notwithstanding the short time we have. It won't be easy, but let's try anyhow.

Friendship makes one lose track of time. We have known each other for thirty-two or thirty-three years and I don't even know whether you are seventy-six or seventy-eight.

HENRY MILLER: Oh, seventy-eight, no, not yet! You keep track well, because you're younger. No, I'm seventy-seven, whatever that means.

You know, I came to youth late in life. I think that it was only after I was forty-five that I started to feel young in the true sense, and I have the impression that at that time I reached a certain level and haven't shifted since.

When I look at myself in the mirror, obviously I know full well that I don't have the face of a man of forty-five, but the spirit is there, and unchanged. Yet when I was young I really felt like an old man. Yes, and that's the case with many young people. Youth is first and foremost a search, a restlessness; you come smack up against everything. You only have to see the idea that the young have of the old; it betrays their own confusion. They see it as a failure, an affliction that brings with it sickness. Many old people who never knew how to be, and never could have been young, see it that way as well, and I should think it's not untrue – for them.

But if you remain open, if you've no fixed ideas, no plans, no ambitions, if you can stay vulnerable always . . .

The more shattered one gets, the more one opens up, that's the important thing.

GEORGES BELMONT: All the same, however young you stay, doesn't this imply that some desires exist which you can no longer satisfy?

HENRY MILLER: Yes, sure. But isn't it one of the illusions of youth to believe that you can do absolutely anything? Nothing is more false, physically, mentally and socially. And what frustrations! But the wisdom that staying young in old age brings is to know that there are limits, that one can do this, but not that; it is being able to control your desires.

The error youth makes is to mistake its desires for realities, and to believe that those desires have no limits. In that way you end up by going against nature. Universal laws exist, laws of the universe; it is madness to want to fight against these laws.

GEORGES BELMONT: As I understand it, you became

young at much the same time as you decided to become a writer. The *Tropic of Cancer*, now that was 1934, as far as I can remember?

HENRY MILLER: Yes, that's right.

GEORGES BELMONT: And yet, the other day I was chatting about you with your secretary, Gerald Robitaille, and happened to remember in passing an anecdote which I had heard before, but which I must confess I'd forgotten: the story of this prayer of yours which you used to say to God, even then, when you were still quite young ...

HENRY MILLER: When I was young – a prayer?

GEORGES BELMONT: Yes, when you were about twenty. A prayer in which you'd say, 'Lord, make me a writer, but make me the best!'

HENRY MILLER: Oh, that's an exaggeration! No, I never asked for that much. It's true that from the age of sixteen up until I was perhaps twenty I still prayed that God would make me a writer – but not 'the best'! No, I never said that. And it was really only a youthful wish, nothing else.

The truth is that I hoped to be, if not another Dostoyevsky, an American Dostoyevsky, or at least to be a little like him. But deep down I knew perfectly well that I couldn't hope to rival Dostoyevsky – he was too remote, he was my idol.

4

GEORGES BELMONT: Was he the only one?

HENRY MILLER: No, there was also Knut Hamsun. For subject-matter, Dostoyevsky, but for style – the style which I should have liked to have attained, which I should have liked to master – it may seem odd, but yes, Knut Hamsun was my ideal.

Even today I often tell myself that I'd really like to be able to write like Hamsun. He is one of the few authors I continue to read again without getting bored. I have read and re-read his book *Mysteries* maybe five times, and each time I still regard it as a masterpiece and say to myself, 'What a pity you can't write like that!'

The curious thing is that the critics should never have thought of Hamsun when they talk about my style – I give them enough hints. I've often been compared with – what's his name, that great Roman writer? – Petronius Arbiter, Petronius of the *Satyricon*. For that matter, they're not far wrong there. Yes, I had my idols I wanted to imitate, and Petronius was the first. After that, of course, there was Rabelais. But never, for instance, Balzac.

GEORGES BELMONT: Never Balzac?

HENRY MILLER: No. He tires me. I don't share the world's opinion of Balzac. Perhaps he's too much, too much of a writer of *novels* – too 'facile', I mean.

I'm always sceptical when an author has a huge output. I distrust a man who is capable of writing something approaching a hundred books. When I was young, I was

told that Balzac had written thirty novels under pseudo-
nyms – nothing under the name of Balzac until the thirty-
first. I'd like to believe that's true; but it's still hard to
believe, isn't it?

GEORGES BELMONT: And yet I can remember when,
before the last war, there was a time when you were always
showering me with letters – not counting the evenings we
used to spend together talking about it – insisting that I
simply had to read one particular book by Balzac.

HENRY MILLER: Oh, really? Which one?

GEORGES BELMONT: *Seraphita.*

HENRY MILLER: Yes, yes, I remember. *Seraphita,* and
Louis Lambert.

GEORGES BELMONT: *Louis Lambert* as well, but above
all *Seraphita,* which I ended up reading, and thanked you
for it. You even wrote an article on *Seraphita.* Surely you
like *that* Balzac?

HENRY MILLER: Certainly. Indeed that was the reason
I wrote that article, *Balzac and his Double.* But I wanted
to explain that Balzac has been false to himself, because
he talks about God and the angel we have in us, and precisely because, in my view, he has nevertheless been false
to the angel.

GEORGES BELMONT: But is the angel present in *Seraphita*?

HENRY MILLER: Yes. Only this book is listed at the beginning of his works. No doubt that's the reason.

Besides, Balzac isn't the only author I can't read. There are other authors and books – *Moby Dick*, now there's one I'll never read. I've tried three or four times, but it's not my sort of thing. A great book, but not my sort of thing.

And Stendhal! I desperately want to get to know Stendhal, but I can't. Impossible.

The same thing goes for Shakespeare. I read him when I was young, but didn't understand any of it. None of it! There's a gap there, sure. However it's a bit late to fill it, I'm afraid.

To tell the truth what I really want to get to know more about right now are the occult authors – maybe. I've read a lot of them already; they attract me. I have retained an appetite for what are known as the Occult Sciences. Is that getting me anywhere? I don't know. But that kind of reading always gives me great pleasure. Almost like sex. It's strange, isn't it? People often say that there are two kinds of book which have no need of publicity: occultist works and pornography, or rather let's say eroticism. And this is true, there's no doubt about it. There's a response there to something within us, for which we hunger.

GEORGES BELMONT: I'd like to get back to your idols. Dostoyevsky I can understand, and Knut Hamsun I knew about, but I'd still like you to be more specific.

HENRY MILLER: Well, in fact I'm not being fair when I speak of Knut Hamsun's style alone. It's difficult to explain, but what I like about him – doubtless because I rather share this ... failing, shall we say – is that his heroines, his women, are always thwarted in love. I've had the same thing in my own life. I mean, I've always been thwarted in that sphere.

GEORGES BELMONT: At first sight that's a pretty surprising picture of you, isn't it? A man thwarted in love? I'm sure that most of your readers wouldn't expect to discover a frustrated man in you. Don't you feel this?

HENRY MILLER: Because I only talk about my sexual loves. But great love, real love, I don't touch on, except perhaps slightly where Mona, the woman who recurs most often in my books, is concerned. But for the rest of them, no. There are girls, or shall we say women, whom I don't mention at all in my writings, don't want to mention, and never will. There's something sacred there. I don't like talking about love in the true sense. Casual affairs are another matter.

And then again I much prefer to show the evil side of myself. My *mauvais côté*, I mean. Yes, I prefer that. The devil instead of the angel.

GEORGES BELMONT: When you speak of Mona – and one does indeed encounter her in almost all your books: in the *Tropic of Capricorn*, in *Sexus*, in that whole huge amalgam which you entitle *The Rosy Crucifixion*, when you call her by this name Mona – I suppose that you do so intentionally, in an almost etymological sense, and that you mean 'the only woman'?

HENRY MILLER: The only woman that I've loved? No, that's inaccurate. By that I mean, yes, in a way you're right. But at the same time, odd as it may seem, I believe that when I'm dying the last image of a woman I shall have will be that of the first – the image of my first love, a young girl.

I was at high school, at the lycée, I don't know what you'd call it here. It was there I met her. I was sixteen and up to the age of twenty I was so in love with her I was in despair. She is still there, in my memory. I can still see her as she was then, totally and exactly. That was frustration in love, great frustration, real torture. But coupled with my image of her is a question equally untouched upon, a problem I have never been able to solve : what this kind of conflict within me over this girl is all about. Meanwhile, she is still my ideal image.

As for Mona, she was a 'real' woman, so to speak, with all the defects and also the qualities of reality. But that first girl was a kind of angel.

GEORGES BELMONT: The first, now she was the one to whom you gave a bunch of violets if I remember right?

HENRY MILLER: Yes, and I dropped them – the flowers that is. I was a very shy young man, you know, extremely shy with girls – with her especially, the first one, because I used to put her on a pedestal, like an idol. It was the age for idols.

The business with the flowers happened the first time I invited her to the theatre. I should think that I've bought flowers on perhaps three occasions in my life, all in all. But that evening was also the very first time I'd done it. Because I was poor we went up to the highest seats in the theatre, in the gods. And just as I was sitting down I let go of the bunch of violets. It fell and she trod on it, by accident of course. But for me it was a fearful symbol; it meant failure, or contempt, or something like that.

GEORGES BELMONT: You mean you thought that she did it on purpose?

HENRY MILLER: Oh, no, not at all. But somehow I interpreted the thing in a Freudian sense.

GEORGES BELMONT: How old were you when this happened?

HENRY MILLER: Oh, about eighteen.

GEORGES BELMONT: Compared with this ideal love, is Mona one woman, or several?

HENRY MILLER: One woman. The others I talk about in my books are always 'one' woman as well. I haven't mixed them up, made composite characters. Each one has a real individuality of her own.

GEORGES BELMONT: It's the real Mona who burns like 'a black crystal star' in the nights of *Tropic of Capricorn*?

HENRY MILLER: Yes.

GEORGES BELMONT: Why does the figure of Mona keep recurring in the most important parts of your work?

HENRY MILLER: Why? Because when I began to write, ten years later ... when I began to write here, in Paris, I wanted to talk about my sufferings during those seven years – yes, only seven years – that I'd lived with her. And I quoted Abelard. Yes, in *Capricorn*, I think, I quoted the words of Abelard who, when speaking of himself, declared that he had suffered more than any man in the world. I thought that I too had suffered as he had – more than any man in the world. And I wanted to talk only of those seven years and nothing else. But some spirit possessed me; you might say I struck out further and further from the shore, despite myself. I just sheered right off.

At the same time, that doesn't prevent everything being closely concentrated into those seven years in my books, enclosed within them, and visibly so. When you think of it, I don't say much about the years that followed. I talk about my childhood, and the years before, but not about the ones after.

GEORGES BELMONT: I'd like to go back – to your prayer beseeching God to make you a writer. How did the idea of writing come to you? It's a trite, silly question, but not unimportant.

HENRY MILLER: How did I decide? That's not easy to say. In one sense, you know, even at the time I was praying to God like that, I wasn't writing a word. I wasn't even trying. No – once I tried to write a page, more like half a page, in pencil, and before I finished I tore up the sheet of paper and said to myself 'You'll never be a writer'. That must have happened – what? – ten years before I tried again.

You know, I became a writer out of a kind of despair – after having tried everything but that. Yes, everything. I had more than a hundred jobs before getting to that stage, and in the end I said to myself, 'You're good for nothing. Why shouldn't you try to be a writer?'

GEORGES BELMONT: That's a pretty original definition of a writer ... When one has tried everything, to say to oneself, 'After all, why not become a writer?'

HENRY MILLER: It certainly is, in a way. All the same, it goes deeper than that. One is born a writer, I think. I've always had that idea.

GEORGES BELMONT: Hence the prayer?

HENRY MILLER: Yes, certainly.

GEORGES BELMONT: There is one thing which is little

known : the story of that first book, *Clipped Wings*, which you never published?

HENRY MILLER : Yes. The manuscript got lost. I left it with my wife June – Mona – and it got lost.

It was a collection of stories, with each one – there were twelve of them – telling the story of a messenger boy. They made up quite a fat book. I'd written it in five weeks.

At that time, I thought that a writer must write for at least twelve hours a day. That was all the more strange because at that time I was working like a slave. Much later on I discovered that two or three hours a day are easily enough and that it's much better that way in every respect. You've got to let it flow until you're empty, and then shut off the faucet.

GEORGES BELMONT : Did you miss this lost manuscript much, and don't you regret its loss? Would one find anything in it anticipating subsequent books?

HENRY MILLER : No, I don't think so. I wrote two other novels after it which weren't published either, and I can find nothing of myself in them. My secretary, Gerald Robitaille, insists that he finds traces, clues, in them. For myself, I don't. They were written by someone else entirely, a completely different person.

GEORGES BELMONT : These two novels followed right after *Clipped Wings*?

HENRY MILLER: Yes, pretty close. I must have written them between 1922 and 1927; that's to say between the ages of thirty-one and thirty-six. Yes, and the oddest thing is that there was one I didn't put my name to, like Balzac. I put my wife's name. There was a man to whom she always said she was a writer ... 'My essays, my short stories'. That was all she talked about. He'd promised her that if she ever showed him a manuscript he'd buy it. She brought him mine; he read it and said, 'It's funny, I'd have sworn that this was written by a man'. But he paid up anyhow, and it was that money that paid for our first trip to Paris, my wife June and I, in 1928.

GEORGES BELMONT: I'd like to know what makes you say it was 'a different person' who'd written those books.

HENRY MILLER: But that's so clear to me! One changes the whole time, don't you think? One's always a different man. Look, for example, I have observed that generally speaking my marriages last seven years. And then again, as I said, when you're young you're searching, you're searching for yourself and you don't find yourself ... until the day you finally do discover yourself. It takes time.

GEORGES BELMONT: Before moving on to Paris, let's stay in New York. The messenger boys in *Clipped Wings*, and the twenties; that was your time with the famous telegraph company, the one featured in *Tropic of Capricorn*, the 'cosmococcic' or 'cosmodemonic' as you call it there?

HENRY MILLER: Yes. It was my period of slavery. A disaster which was full of riches – like Siberia for Dostoyevsky. In other words, a fund of treasure.

I stayed there for four and a half years. At first as a messenger too. But at the same time, I'm not ashamed to say, as a kind of spy. I had the job of checking whether the other messengers, particularly the young ones, were well treated, or if the bosses in the various offices bullied them. I was sacked twice because I was thought to be too easygoing. But the managing director trusted me. He changed my duties, and I acted as personnel manager.

It was surrealistic. Imagine it: every day I used to see a hundred or so characters troop past me, because we were in constant need of stop gaps. I'd take on twenty or thirty, but judging a hundred cases every day! And reading all those references! Often they were phoney. You'd see the lot, even thieves. We'd sign on boys of fourteen and old men of seventy.

For me, it was a marvellous, exhausting human experience. The day over, I'd wait for the security man on duty to arrive, and after a snack we'd make a tour of the offices together – there were approximately a hundred of those, too. We used to visit about thirty. We became very friendly, the security man and I. He'd open the till, check the accounts, and make an inspection. It was crazy, the fiddles he'd unearth!

The men they employed were the scum of the earth, especially the ones between twenty and thirty. This was after the First World War, don't forget. There were a lot of veterans among them, some disabled, some even blind.

They used to earn nothing and I myself was always broke because I'd give them money; I even used to borrow from other people, my staff, to hand it out. But behind each of these men was a story . . . always some horrifying story! They'd stay standing and I'd say to them, 'Have a chair, sit down and go right ahead, tell me your story'. And often the man would start to cry and sob; it was worse than being a psychoanalyst. The former personnel manager, whom I had replaced had been kept on in an inferior post and was just nearby. He kept saying, 'Miller, don't waste your time with those guys', but I'd reply, 'I'm not wasting my time; on the contrary . . .', and it was true.

GEORGES BELMONT: And what made you leave the job?

HENRY MILLER: The decision to become a writer. Mona, my wife at that time, insisted on it.

One day, without thinking twice about it, I turned up for work; there were the usual hundred or so applicants. I told my secretary, 'Telephone the Management and tell them I'm sick of it, I'm quitting; they can keep the two weeks salary they owe me, I don't give a damn about it'. And I scooped up my papers, picked up my briefcase and my hat, and left. In the street, I remember I walked like a free man coming out of Siberia.

After that, another miserable existence began. I have told the story of how, with Mona, we tried to sell my writings, printed on lousy paper, in Greenwich Village and Second Avenue cafés. That didn't work. Then we tried imported candies . . . two suitcases full we used to drag around. It was tough. I'd stay outside, she'd go into the cafés. Sometimes she'd come out with a fifty dollar bill; a man had said, 'I'll take the lot!' But on other days we would sell nothing, and there was snow, rain, and cold feet. And standing outside as always, with soaking, frozen feet, I'd get to thinking, 'That bitch! Where's she got to? What in hell is she up to in that bar?' A weird life!

I thought I was the most wretched man in the world. It wasn't true; the wretchedness wasn't over. It reached its peak in Paris. Only it wasn't the same sort of wretchedness. It had, you might say, more savour. Suffer as I might, there was the atmosphere of the place, the people. Everything was different. Yes, even suffering was becoming almost pleasant. And above all, in Paris, a kind of simplification occurred within me.

Not long ago, I found a letter which was intended for my best friend at that time, the time I'd begun to write in New York. Today I blush when I re-read it. What a vocabulary! I was in love with words. I thought that being a great writer meant using great words. And every time I sat down at my typewriter I had in front of me, on the walls, spread round me, everywhere, all the words that I wanted to slot into what I was writing. And I'd shove them all in, willy-nilly, the lot of them! Today I laugh over it, it was so ridiculous.

But in Paris I changed. And the change didn't come only from myself. For a start I read a lot of French books, in which I found the economy of expression that I lacked. The style of my letters to my friends became different, which was one sign of this. I no longer sent them 'writerish' letters.

And then again, the pictorial side of Paris struck me

greatly. It's a queer thing, but at the time of my first visit as a tourist I had been insensitive to this side of the city; in fact on that occasion Paris had hardly attracted me at all – less than Budapest, for instance. There had to be a second time, a time when I was totally broke, desperate, and living on the streets like a tramp, for me to begin to see the real Paris and to love it, discover it at the same time as discovering myself.

I can recall the old dilapidated, defaced walls. I used to see real-life paintings everywhere. And I began to write as one paints a picture – in order to depict things.

I think there has always been a little of the painter in me. I was already doing water-colours in New York before that. To be frank, I only became a writer in the third instance. I began with music, the piano. I was passionately fond of the piano, the organ, and also the harp, even though I've never played it. Even today I rate music above all the arts. After that there was painting, and finally writing. And for that, as I say, I owe much to Paris.

Oh, I didn't do it alone. I reached rock bottom in Paris. Even when my first books were published I was far from surfacing. *Tropic of Cancer* was almost a flop. But I refused to accept failure. I did all that I could on my own, personally, so that the world should know I had written a good book. I'm rather ashamed to relate this now, but I was like a mother who has brought a child into the world and doesn't want to lose it; I fought to protect it. You know that my astrological sign is Capricorn, and they say that this sign gives you a very practical side to your nature. I am a bit of a businessman in my way.

During that period I bombarded people with stacks of letters. I remember that the first was to the petty monarch of some remote little island – I forget the name. One of my friends knew this kinglet, and during the night I got up to write this letter. Peculiar idea, eh?

Later I started the whole caper again for another of my books, *Sunday After the War,* which I'd published here at my own expense. It was a limited edition, but even after selling sixty or so copies there were still plenty left and I was furious. So, one night a friend of mine and I were both pretty drunk, and I said, 'Why not send out the unsold copies to strangers? Hand me the telephone book.' And we sent out several hundred volumes into the blue, just like that. I didn't even keep one for myself. It's taken me thirty years or so to find a single copy!

All the same, the most curious thing, when I look back on those difficult times, is that it should be my youth in New York or, later on, my years in Paris . . . the most curious thing, is that I've the impression I've always kept my eyes wide open – my ears too. I used to pay great attention to whatever anyone said to me, and I used to look . . . my eyes would gobble things up. And I still do this today. On reflection, it's probably a way of preparing to become a writer . . . or perhaps a reporter rather than a writer.

GEORGES BELMONT : No, more than a reporter, because it's also a way of listening in to yourself.

HENRY MILLER : Myself? Do you think so?

GEORGES BELMONT: Yes. The least that one can say is that you have an awe-inspiring facility for hearing the world's echo, and that of other people, in your own inner resonance.

HENRY MILLER: Yes, that's true. However, there was a period, you know – my youth – when I was horribly arrogant, yes, that's the word . . . supercilious, scornful, haughty. I used to despise other people; I'd have liked to have been able to change the world. But as I wrote I changed my ideas – and how!

Today I've no longer the slightest wish to change the world. When I am at peace and feel on good terms with myself, calm, tranquil, I say to myself, 'Maybe, after all, the world is all right as it is?' If you lay a finger on it – a finger here, a finger there – you end up confused. How can you expect one man to change the world with all its ills?

To some extent I have accepted the human condition, and I don't think that's compromising, either. I hope it's wisdom that makes me say that. Other people say, 'Ah, now that he's old he's become resigned; he accepts it all because he's impotent. I don't believe any of that myself.

GEORGES BELMONT: What is striking about your work, in fact, is that what you call acceptance of the world has no hint of passive acceptance, either of things, society, or individuals. On the contrary it seems to me to be an extremely active, generous acceptance of everything: life, things in general, and in particular human beings.

HENRY MILLER: And even of my enemies. And that I reckon is the most important thing, because it's said – and rightly so – that the enemy is within, inside you, and not outside.

I have finally absorbed this fact and understand that I myself am the enemy as well. Likewise, in my view, it is very important to accept the 'other', the person who is not *for* you. This is why I like St Francis of Assisi so much . . . because he accepted everything, up to and including atheists. In a way I find him better than Jesus.

GEORGES BELMONT: That is precisely what I call your generous acceptance of the world.

There's one question which readers of your work often put to me. It's this: 'Do the people who live and speak in his books (for one *is* directly involved with life and speech in them, and one has the impression of being immersed in lives as they are lived, and in words as they are really spoken), do these characters really exist, or did they exist the way they're described? What have you to say to that?

HENRY MILLER: Why, yes, they really were like they are in my books. Sometimes of course there is a distortion, an exaggeration, but this is more to bring out the truth; not to disguise things, but to go into them in depth.

When a man speaks to you, there are a great many things behind what he says that are important. That is what I try to put across. Not only the talk but what is behind it, whether concealed spontaneously or not.

GEORGES BELMONT: What seems to me of prime importance – and I remember this was one of the first things I thought of when reading your books in the past – is that this desire to get inside people comes, in your case, not from curiosity, but from integrity . . . that above all it comes from the heart. The heart is essential in your work. It's heart that leads you to inflate, to exaggerate aspects of someone that are often only potentially present in him.

HENRY MILLER: Yes, I think that's true.

GEORGES BELMONT: You act as a revealer of people.

I remember that two years ago I was in New York and one evening I met a professor from an American university. A short time before this he had himself met one of your characters at a friend's house . . . a character, incidentally, from what you told me was a favourite among your own books: *The Colossus of Maroussi*. The name of this character is Katsimbalis. He is the 'colossus'. And he too now has a professorship at an American university, in Florida I believe. And this other professor who had met him told me most ingenuously, and I'm sure with the greatest of honesty, that he recognized nothing of your 'colossus' in Katsimbalis. He was very disappointed.

HENRY MILLER: Wasn't that *his* fault? Not Katsimbalis', nor mine.

GEORGES BELMONT: Doubtless. Nevertheless it is a fact that you have a tendency — once again through generosity — to exaggerate your subjects, to exaggerate what seems to you to be the best and richest sides of them.

HENRY MILLER: Yes, that's true enough — at least as far as characters I like are concerned.

You know, there is one thing in life that upsets and distresses me about people: it's that they never want to acknowledge greatness in others. They always want to demean... 'A giant? Oh no, not a chance! Impossible!'

Having said that, perhaps I also exaggerate the characters I don't like, but in the opposite way.

GEORGES BELMONT: I wonder. In fact, I doubt that one could discover a trace of malice in your books; I don't feel that any of them portray someone over-drawn in a derogatory way.

HENRY MILLER: Perhaps the price I make others pay — those whom I don't like, or feel contempt for, or even hate — is that I often portray them in caricature. I have often been told that I excel in caricature, and that's certainly true! It seems to me that I always see things in two ways : in reality and in caricature.

GEORGES BELMONT : For my part, I submit that even your caricatures come from the heart.

I am thinking, for instance, of a kind of character who appears fairly constantly throughout your books in one guise or another, and whom I shall typify as your Doctor Kronsky, the rather grotesque psychoanalyst whom you end up by psychoanalysing yourself, making him cough up to his patients all the money he'd taken from them. You surround him with an aura of such affection, for all his grotesqueness, and embellish him to the point of such opulence, that in his way he's no longer grotesque at all. Or am I wrong?

HENRY MILLER : First, I'm going to tell you one thing : I don't much like psychoanalysts, even the greatest. Jung, for example . . . for me he's a great awful bore. In one sense I respect him, for his explorations; he had some brilliant ideas, but he sticks in one's crop, and he's so ponderous . . ! Ah, yes, he's a real Swiss! And Freud! I read all I could of him, as well as Jung and the rest of them, when I was young, and I was thrilled by it. But nowadays that means nothing to me any more. They tell me, apropos of Freud, that he 'broke down the barriers'. I don't agree at all. In my opinion he made a good job of dumping new loads on us and our consciences. He has liberated one side of us, and over-burdened the other. We're barely hobbling along.

GEORGES BELMONT : At least it's true to say that Oedipus didn't have a complex.

HENRY MILLER: There you are!

As for my Doctor Kronsky, he really was grotesque in real life. Only he was very goodhearted. I met him at the Telegraph Company, and we became friends at once. He was part of the huge circle of friends I had at that period. He wasn't a messenger boy, he was a medical student. I was fond of him because he was grotesque and because he had great heart. He would often criticize me. It even got to the point where we'd spar in the street when we were discussing things of an evening. He'd put up his mitts and invite me to do the same. And we'd spar away. The oddest thing was that I was his boss, his *patron*.

Later, at a time when I'd decided at all costs to commit suicide, he gave me a pill – out of goodheartedness. For a whole year I'd kept on begging him, 'Give me something so that I can have done with it and kill myself'. He'd reply, 'Come on now, that's no sort of a thing to do'. And then one day he said to me, 'Well, all right, since you're set on it, here you are'. And he handed me a pill. . . . You know the story?

GEORGES BELMONT: I'd like you to tell it, anyhow.

HENRY MILLER: Well, I swallowed his pill, then I took off all my clothes. I was lying naked on the bed. It was the middle of winter. I opened the window to make sure of doing the job properly. During the night it began to snow. When I opened my eyes in the morning I hadn't even caught a cold, but because the window was open I was covered with snow. The bugger had slipped me a sleeping-pill!

GEORGES BELMONT: Where did this obsession with suicide come from?

HENRY MILLER: Oh, from my hassles with Mona, my failure as a writer, my relations with my parents – everything. Everything was desolation, sadness . . . disappointment after disappointment.

You know, not long ago in Venice I thought about committing suicide again. From time to time it gets me. But now I've got used to it. I tell myself, 'Right, here we go again! . . .' And I think about how I didn't kill myself the other times, and how I'll surely find a way of riding it out again, you see? So, I go to bed and tell myself that I'll stay there until it's over. Sometimes I stay there twenty-four or forty-eight hours at a stretch. When it's over I get up, I feel good, and I'm hungry – a sure sign of good health!

GEORGES BELMONT: Being in good health has always been important to you?

HENRY MILLER: Essential.

GEORGES BELMONT: Of prime importance, even?

HENRY MILLER: Yes.

GEORGES BELMONT: Do you still dose yourself with spoonfuls of liquid paraffin every morning? You used to in the past.

HENRY MILLER: Yes, because I was constipated. But that
went away a long time ago. You know how?

There was a doctor who swore that he could cure me.
I said, 'Thanks a lot. What do I have to do?' He replied,
'Don't think about it, even if it comes back, take absolutely
no notice of it and it will go away of its own accord.'

I thought it over and it came to me: the remedy is not
to worry about it. And that's what I did in the worst
disasters – even where constipation wasn't concerned. I
stayed impassive, like a Buddha.

GEORGES BELMONT: And that was enough?

HENRY MILLER: Yes, that's all it takes.

GEORGES BELMONT: Just now you seemed to imply that
you'd suffered from a feeling of frustration even in your
relationship with your parents. What was that relationship?

HENRY MILLER: Above all it was my relationship with my
mother. She didn't love me. The neighbours say the opposite
– that she loved me very much. In any case she never
showed me any affection. She never kissed me once. All
the time she used to insist that I was a failure, a good-for-
nothing, a worthless character. And also that I always
missed out on everything. So much so that by criticizing
me, she undermined my very spirit. Try as I would, she
never expressed a hint of joy over what I did. For her I
never did anything right, nor anything good. When I decided to become a writer, she was somehow hurt. In her

view it was pure madness. She wanted me to be a tailor and work with my father. Now *that* was madness, stupidity.

From the age of sixteen on, as far as I can recall, the curtain was down between us. My only satisfaction was that she left me entirely free. I could play around in the street until all hours. As a young kid I was already coming home late at night; they never asked me what I'd been up to.

After that I left home. I lived with the woman whom I have depicted as 'the Widow'. She was my mother's age, or nearly. She had a son a year older than myself. Pretty good, eh?

And then I came back home, probably because I was out of money and out of work. I was unable to go on living with that woman. Yes, I went back, and for a period of five or six weeks I tried to write.

I had my typewriter, and I'd tap away on it. And every time a neighbour, male or female, rapped on the window or rang the doorbell my mother would come rushing in and say to me: 'Quick, Henry, quick! Hide your typewriter, and get into the cupboard!' And then . . . oh, the smell of camphor and naphthalene! There were times when I'd stay shut in there for an hour, sometimes two, because my mother didn't want anyone to know that her son was writing. To her it was something shameful.

Over the years she has never read a line of anything I've written. She didn't want to hear even a mention of my books. When, at a much later date, I visited my mother and father, that was the kind of thing one didn't talk about . . . taboo! Only once, after my return from France in 1940, she

asked me : 'Have you made any money?' I answered that
I hadn't and that it was better not to talk about it. Then she
said to me, 'Why haven't you at least written a book like
Gone with the Wind?' Think of it, what a woman, eh?

GEORGES BELMONT : Do you think this attitude your
mother had could have had any effect, however momentary,
on your own attitude towards women in general?

HENRY MILLER : I am often asked that. Yes, many people
say so. I suppose there's a half-truth there. Nothing is as
terrible as not feeling loved by one's mother, and feeling no
love for her – nothing, not even filial respect.

I have described in my books the way she treated my
sister, who was backward. Instead of showing her affection,
understanding and sympathy, she was constantly punishing
her.

I must have been eight when she began to give her
lessons, because the school didn't want to take her – she was
impossible, too 'retarded'. I was going to school myself and
in the evening I used to do my homework in the kitchen.
There was a blackboard there. When my mother decided
to teach my sister arithmetic I remember she'd say, for
instance, 'What do one and two make?' My sister would
reply 'Five'. Then my mother : 'No wrong!' My sister
would say 'Seven', and so on. In the end she'd become
hysterical and would blurt out any number. And each time
she did so my mother would give her a slap. And there I
was sitting over my exercise books and schoolbooks, taking
it all in. It was . . . I'd sweat like mad . . .

GEORGES BELMONT: Your sister was older than you?

HENRY MILLER: No. Four years younger. And she was an angel. An angel in the real sense, and she's always stayed one. She has never known envy, hypocrisy, lies – none of that. Yes, she really was an angel. She had a nature of the utmost goodness but, like angels, she was not made to live in this world.

GEORGES BELMONT: And your father?

HENRY MILLER: Oh, he's something else entirely. When I was young I didn't much like him either, because he caused me pain. Every night he'd come home drunk and have constant rows with my mother. There were always scenes at supper, and it wasn't long before the two of them would start to scrap. And I'd begin to gag. It's a disorder I've suffered from for years; I'd start eating and my throat would get constricted. That lasted a long time.

But later, much later, when I came back from France and saw my father again and we chatted together, I discovered that he was a good man, a very good man. It was my mother who plagued him; she'd criticized him all his life. I really think that she was the cause of everything.

GEORGES BELMONT: And how did your father react vis-à-vis your books?

HENRY MILLER: Oh, he was always happy to know that

I'd written a new book, even though he'd only read one of them, *Money and how it gets this way*.

GEORGES BELMONT: That little pamphlet you published yourself in Paris, before the war?

HENRY MILLER: That's it. And he thought that everything I said in it about money was the truth. And yet it was a satire, a burlesque even, or something near it. But he used to take it dead seriously.

And there's another of his quirks I remember. He'd read one other book, just one, in his whole life. I defy anyone to guess what it was. It was Ruskin's *The Stones of Venice*, which I myself find difficult reading. Why on earth that particular one! I still wonder. But he literally adored it.

GEORGES BELMONT: Did you yourself read much when you were a child?

HENRY MILLER: Oh, yes. I always had a book in front of me from the time I began to learn to read onwards. My grandfather was a tailor, like my father. I can still see him sitting crosslegged, sewing on his low table, and I'd sit down beside him and read – I was six or seven. My mother would lecture him about it, and say, 'You shouldn't allow that child to read like that; it's very bad for him'.

GEORGES BELMONT: What sort of books did you read at that age? Children's books, I assume?

HENRY MILLER: Of course. I was no genius, you know. But when I was about sixteen, I began to immerse myself in all the great authors. Yes . . . even Balzac!

I remember I read *La Peau de Chagrin* in English. In translation the title became *The Wild Ass Skin*. But there was a snag. In English, as you know, the word 'ass' does mean 'donkey' but also 'backside', and when my father saw the title he forbade me to bring such books into the house. He figured that it was some pornographic dime-novel.

GEORGES BELMONT: At dinner the other night you told me that you were at present re-reading certain books from your childhood?

HENRY MILLER: From my childhood? Not really, no. Mostly from my early years in Paris. The Salavin stories by Georges Duhamel: *La Confession de Minuit, Le Journal de Salavin*. And also . . . oh, I forget . . .

GEORGES BELMONT: But cast your mind back. You told me about a book and we realized that we'd both read it when we were children . . . *Cuore* [*Heart*] by an Italian author, Edmundo de Amici, I think, who is completely forgotten these days, I fear.

HENRY MILLER: Ah yes, you're right. I re-read it six months ago. The idea just came to me out of the blue. Why, I don't know.

These days I get a stronger and stronger urge to know what used to appeal to me in my youth. At the time I was full of admiration for this or that author, and I like to compare whatever I may think of him now with what I felt for him in the past. The most bizarre thing is that in that respect I've not changed at all : I still admire these authors as much now as then. It's extremely reassuring to discover that, you know.

GEORGES BELMONT : You don't think that you admire these books because, as with your own characters, you transform them and add something to them? . . . That you add, perhaps, something of yourself, in the final analysis?

HENRY MILLER : No, no, I admire them for themselves. Take, for instance an author like Rider Haggard – an American writer for children and young people who is little known in this country, a kind of Mayne Reid. I've re-read him. Some of his works really are great books. But everyone laughs at me when I say that. 'That's for the kids', they tell me, but I don't think so. Mind you, it's a fact that he's no longer popular with young people in the States nowadays. The same goes for Jack London; he's not read much any more. And there's someone else whom I liked enormously, especially for his revolutionary feeling – he was a socialist at a time when that was frowned on. He was treated as a 'radical', as an extremist, or near-extremist. I forget his name . . . wait . . . no, I've got it : Dreiser.

GEORGES BELMONT : What lead you to read Salavin again? Chance?

HENRY MILLER: Yes, in a sense. One day I went for a stroll in the Rue Mouffetard and the Place de la Contrescarpe; I went back later, and on one of those jaunts I suddenly remembered that in Duhamel's book Salavin had lived in the Rue du Pot-de-fer, just nearby. So I thought, 'Well, now I must re-read the story of Salavin'.

The funniest part of it is that I don't know why I got the feeling – which proves how much my first reading of it struck me. I had the feeling that the opening sentence of the book was '*Je me nomme Louis Salavin. . .*' . But I couldn't find that sentence in the *Confession de Minuit* which I'd just bought. I got really quite disturbed and uneasy; and kept thinking, 'My word, Duhamel has cut that sentence from the later editions; why the hell?' And I floundered around trying to think why. Later on I found it; it was in the *Journal*. Then I was happy.

GEORGES BELMONT: How did that second reading of it impress you?

HENRY MILLER: Very forcibly. It's a work of great simplicity, in my opinion, and not really French in feel; Russian, rather, as though Duhamel had been influenced by the great Russian writers.

Salavin is an ordinary man, almost a failure, but he's only a failure in the world's view of him, not the reader's. On the contrary, for the reader he's a very interesting character who reveals every side of himself. That's what appeals to me.

GEORGES BELMONT: You mean that he's like so many of Dostoyevsky's characters who are failures in terms of their lives, but who make, one might say, exciting reading?

HENRY MILLER: Exactly. That's why I say that there's an analogy between Duhamel and the Russians.

GEORGES BELMONT: Do you find that you've a special affection for failures?

HENRY MILLER: Yes. For poor people, failures, the wretched of the earth, everyone like that. More so than for men who are recognized and famous. And for the good reason that I tell myself that I too am still nothing but a failure. I always identify with these people. For the most part I've been a failure all my life, I think. And even today, I still wonder . . .

GEORGES BELMONT: Aren't you exaggerating rather?

HENRY MILLER: Perhaps, perhaps, but that's how I feel. I can't get the idea out of my head, do you see?

GEORGES BELMONT: All the same, hasn't there been a moment in your life and in your work when, as a writer especially, you felt somehow certain of yourself and what you were doing? Or have you perhaps always doubted yourself a lot?

HENRY MILLER: No, it would be wrong to assert that I

always have doubts. For instance I am now starting to believe in what I'm doing, and basically, I was certain quite early on. Yes, I think I can say this – even outside my books, being certain about what I am and my ideas generally, a strong feeling of certainty, even. I've always fought against 'knowledge', against intellectuals. That's what's important. In my opinion, intelligence alone leads nowhere and intellectuals can never be certain of anything. They're men who are always doubting. They talk as though they 'know' but they don't know – at least I don't think so. Whereas a very simple man who is, let's say, rather religious in temperament, can have that certainty. And for me it's a marvellous thing to meet human beings like that.

GEORGES BELMONT: You have just used the word 'religious'. Now, there are passages in one of your books, one which I think reveals quite a lot about what people call your philosophy – forgive the expression, I know you don't like it much when applied to yourself – certain passages in *The World of Sex*, to call it by its name, in which you insist on the fact that you are a religious man. Could you explain what you mean by that?

HENRY MILLER: There's nothing I'd like better. It's a subject which concerns me all the more intimately because most people don't believe that I could be religious. Nevertheless, I am. That doesn't prevent me from disliking all religions. To me all religions are idiotic, and a bad thing for mankind.

At the same time I do believe in certain things. It's

difficult to explain. Fundamentally I am a religious man without a religion. I believe in the existence of a Supreme Intelligence . . . call it God if you like. I believe there is a bond between myself and this God who is bound with the cosmos. But I also believe it to be a fact that we shall never *know*, we shall never penetrate into the mystery of life. That's a thing you've got to accept, and in that sense I am religious.

I've no need of 'texts'. The Churches, even Buddhism, are only a travesty of religion in my opinion. Often, one is right in calling oneself more religious, more of a believer in that sense, than many who claim they are.

I believe that chance does not exist in the universe, everything follows rules. Life has great significance. If you haven't absorbed that fact, it's not worth a thing, not worth speaking about. The important thing is that man should never lose sight of his link with the universe. Life is a miracle. For me, everything is mystery and miracle. I can't be realistic about life, like so many young people are. For me it is the sacred, holy thing.

GEORGES BELMONT: You've just used the word 'cosmos'. I think that one of the most striking features of your work is that the religious side of you is expressed to the fullest extent – too bad if this term sounds a bit ridiculous nowadays, it still has a meaning – by a sort of pantheism. Your books are shot through with sudden illuminating moments. For example, in the *Tropic of Capricorn* there is an unforgettable passage where you are in a forest, you've been for a swim, and go into a cabin to change.

HENRY MILLER: Ah, yes!

GEORGES BELMONT: And at that moment a fantastic storm breaks out; you go out into the rain, with the lightning flashing all around you, and indulge in a kind of ritual dance – I can't think of another way of putting it. I refuse to believe that that passage was pure invention?

HENRY MILLER: No, it really happened.

GEORGES BELMONT: And you called on God . . .

HENRY MILLER: Yes, but I denied him!

GEORGES BELMONT: More than that: you reviled him.

HENRY MILLER: Yes.

GEORGES BELMONT: Just as the ancient Greeks were able to revile their gods.

HENRY MILLER: Yes. What about it? Does the passage seem hard to swallow?

GEORGES BELMONT: Certainly not. On the contrary I see it as a supreme manifestation of your religious feeling, of that union, or at the very least, that bond with the cosmos you were speaking of a moment ago.

□□□□

HENRY MILLER: You know the other evening I ran into Brassai, the photographer who is writing a book about me. We talked, and I put this question to him: 'Do you find contradictions in my books, in what I say in them?' He answered, 'But you are nothing but a mass of contradictions! You contradict yourself in everything you talk about.' And that's quite possible.

Walt Whitman said the same about himself: 'Do I contradict myself? Well then, true, I contradict myself; so what?'

GEORGES BELMONT: And Gide used to say, 'Only fools don't contradict themselves.'

HENRY MILLER: Quite right. What does contradiction mean? Nothing. In relation to truth, I mean. Every human being is made up of contradictions.

GEORGES BELMONT: You also used the word 'realist' just now. There are often people who, when they talk about your books, maintain that you are a realist. What do you think?

HENRY MILLER: No, I don't think I'm a realist, nor a surrealist for that matter. I've a certain idea of reality, but I still say that the reality I talk about is spelt with a capital 'R'.

But I dislike realist authors because I find that their sort of realism, without being precisely a lie, is just an imitation of true reality. It's just the surface of things, do you see? Just superficial. Their realism never takes one right into the truth of reality. You're just served up with facts, and for my part I believe that these facts say nothing in themselves. What is important is the interpretation of the facts.

GEORGES BELMONT: In other words your reality, with a capital 'R', is an interpretation? It has nothing to do with what people these days call objective reality?

HENRY MILLER: Certainly not.

GEORGES BELMONT: It's a subjective reality?

HENRY MILLER: Yes. And I know it's impossible to supply a definition of that sort of reality. It comes from experience. It *is* experience. When you talk about it, when you express it in that sense, you're certain you're right. No need to look for a definition, for the good reason that there are very few people who are, or are capable of being, that certain.

GEORGES BELMONT: In this connection, it seems to me that one of the most suprising things about you, and something which, as you well know, makes many intellectuals, as you were saying just now, not understand your thoughts and not even attempt to do so, often tending to dismiss it as a kind of naïvety . . .

HENRY MILLER: Naïvety! Yes, that's exactly the term they use, 'naïve'. It's a fact.

Often people think that I borrow from all the great philosophers. And yet the oddest thing is that I've never digested the ideas of philosophers. I've tried – all the philosophers, all the greatest ones – and I end up getting totally confused; I really don't understand any of it, and keep on telling myself that philosophy is not for daily consumption, not for everyday living, it's something abstract and divorced from our lives as we really live them now. You can't *live* a philosophy.

To put it plainly, my philosophy, if I've got one, is a philosophy of non-philosophy.

GEORGES BELMONT: Personally speaking, I consider that your 'philosophy', in quotes, is first and foremost a sort of art of living, much more than the result of abstract thought.

HENRY MILLER: Yes. That is, I'd like it to be that way. That's why I have such profound admiration for the ancient Chinese. They possessed the art of interpretation, or rather discrimination – that's a much better word, discrimination – the art of discrimination. And I think that that is real wisdom. They have never been religious, those Chinese, but they knew how to live. There you are.

GEORGES BELMONT: You mean that they knew how to live because they knew how to choose?

HENRY MILLER: Yes.

GEORGES BELMONT: That's what you mean by discrimination?

HENRY MILLER: Yes.

GEORGES BELMONT: To be selective in life is the art of living, then? The art is of necessity in the choosing?

HENRY MILLER: You know, there's a Chinese paradox which runs something like this: 'If the wrong man says the right thing, it does not mean anything' . . . isn't the truth, in other words.

GEORGES BELMONT: What route, and I'd like you to explain this because I know the great attachment you have for it in your thinking, led you to discover Oriental philosophy – Zen, for instance? Was it by chance?

HENRY MILLER: No. It all began when I was seventeen, and discovered Lao-Tse. I forget exactly how his book came into my hands, but for me that was the starting-point. In Brooklyn, I ask you! It's incredible. Me reading Lao-Tse in the middle of that crazy family! When I come to think of it, it was a really cockeyed situation.

GEORGES BELMONT: But it wasn't chance?

HENRY MILLER: No, I've told you, I don't believe chance exists. People are always talking about chance, coincidence, but that's not it. In my opinion it's destiny.

Anyway, when I read Lao-Tse, I swept away all other philosophies. Even today I still consider his book a very, very great book, one of the greatest in the world. And yet it's a really thin volume. But what a lesson there is to learn there; look at the way everything can be said in a few lines!

Perhaps there's also something Oriental in my nature; I think so. I feel an equal affinity with the Chinese, the Japanese, the Hindus and the Indians, even if they do contradict each other. I can still find features in each one of them, a sustenance which gives me pleasure... A real affinity.

GEORGES BELMONT: In the past you used to tell me that it was your dream to go off to Tibet?

HENRY MILLER: That's true.

GEORGES BELMONT: Once, before the war, you even announced to me that towards the end of your life you'd set off for that part of the world and when you got there you wouldn't die, you'd just disappear, vanish into the air.

HENRY MILLER: Yes, I remember that well. At that time I had the idea well and truly fixed in my mind. But I don't believe in it any more. By way of consolation I tell myself that I've already been there.

GEORGES BELMONT: In spirit?

HENRY MILLER: Yes, in a sense. And there's some truth in

it. Why not? It seems to me that one can easily have a psychic or spiritual experience without the need to confine oneself physically or geographically.

GEORGES BELMONT: You mean that you have a Tibet within?

HENRY MILLER: Yes, that's it.

GEORGES BELMONT: Then what is death to you nowadays? Another dimension of life?

HENRY MILLER: The truth is, no one knows anything about death. They talk about it. It's a word – a word which fills a void, because we have no idea what it means. But personally, I believe there is no death.

GEORGES BELMONT: Is that because you believe in metempsychosis?

HENRY MILLER: When I read books on reincarnation the notion seems to me very plausible, but no more than that. I can't very well decide whether it's true or not. Besides, I don't feel that thinking about oneself *after* is important; one life is enough. As for proving reincarnation, it's impossible. I know that there are people who state positively that it exists; but it's a very hard thing to understand in general terms.

GEORGES BELMONT: After reading your books one is left

with the impression that you have lived through several deaths. Aren't you in fact talking about a form of reincarnation in life? Is that what the word *re-birth* means for you?

HENRY MILLER: Re-birth? Yes, I have died several times, many times. And my re-births are a real experience, which I feel strongly.

Here, you are getting into a different territory. Religion aside, I believe that one can interpret the resurrection of Jesus in precisely this way. It's not merely a question of life, death, and heaven. One can come back to life without physically dying. My life is full of resurrections . . .

GEORGES BELMONT: If you were asked, at the present stage in your resurrections, to summarize what you think is the art of living, what would you say?

HENRY MILLER: I think that today my ideal, and true wisdom, is to do less and less in every sphere – floating instead of swimming. Life seems to me to be such a simple matter that I wonder why I have ever felt the need to do anything. Why react? I just keep buoyant, as swimmers say. Yes, I just keep buoyant, because what is all this turmoil in the world but a sign of the great malaise within people? All outside events – social problems, for example – derive from this state of agitation. If one becomes a simple man, a wise man, social problems vanish. Our internal jitters create them.

As an American, I am in a good position to see what a

gross caricature this activity is. That sort of activity's fit for insects. When you watch insects going about their business, you catch yourself thinking: why are they rushing around so much? What are they *doing*? . . . But most of all: why? . . . They're always so busy and preoccupied it seems laughable to us. However when we look at ourselves, we don't find each other laughable. But in my view, we are.

GEORGES BELMONT: One gets the impression, notably from your two great initial eruptions into literature – the two *Tropics* – that it's precisely the sense of absurdity in human activity which, perhaps, helped you to become a writer.

HENRY MILLER: Absurdity, yes, of course. These days it's become a great word. People talk about nothing but the 'theatre of the absurd', and the 'literature of the absurd'. But this sort of literature doesn't exactly correspond with the ideas on the subject I had then. No, I was thinking more, perhaps, of evil – the absurdity of evil; of the fact that one can kill in war, for example. I shall never understand how a man can make war. I can forgive a man who kills out of passion, for personal reasons, but to go out en masse and shoot at just anybody! . . . When I see that, I say that we're not human beings yet and that we shall not be as long as war is not abolished.

Perhaps that's my private utopia, but I don't think so. For instance, I can live in peace, even with my enemies. What prevents other people from doing the same? As I see it, it's within the realms of possibility. We've certainly seen great men live this way.

GEORGES BELMONT: But things usually turned out badly for them, you must admit.

HENRY MILLER: You mean that in many cases they are martyrs?

GEORGES BELMONT: Yes, look at Christ and Gandhi.

HENRY MILLER: Doubtless, but it's not a general rule. For me, there's a difference between religious sensibility and wisdom. Wise men are not obliged to become martyrs to the same extent. If that happens to them it's the fault of 'men of religion', because they want to make conversions. They are hard, arrogant; they want to compel others to adopt their beliefs.

GEORGES BELMONT: Is that the difference between Mohammed and Buddha? Do you prefer Buddha?

HENRY MILLER: Certainly. But nowadays, when I read Zen, for example, I realize how ridiculous it is to worship *one* Buddha, because Zen teaches us that we are *all* Buddhas. If one recognizes the fact that one is, or at least has the ability to become a Buddha, it's wrong to strain piety to the point of worshipping just one. To get to that point constitutes a defeat because on close analysis one realizes that what one is really doing is setting up an idol on nothing, and there is a vast rift between the idol and this nothingness, a difference that can never be resolved.

I often say that one mustn't go into raptures over geniuses, nor pay homage to saints, nor condemn criminals, 'other people' . . . It seems to me that one does what one can in life. Life is, perhaps, a huge orchestra in which each of us has his part of the score to play. The only important thing is that each of us should play his own part, whatever it may be. It's funny, and on the other hand it's not funny, but tragic, even, and amounts to saying 'If you're a murderer, do it well'.

GEORGES BELMONT: Do you feel that one can determine the part, that one can choose it?

HENRY MILLER: No, I don't think so. I believe it is *given* to us.

Bearing that in mind, most people don't even realize that they're playing a part. They aren't actors in the real sense. They are quite content just to react. They have no character, not even destinies. It's not important what they do, nor what becomes of them. Don't misunderstand me: I don't say that out of indifference or contempt on my part. It's simply a reality.

GEORGES BELMONT: I'd like to get back to Zen, and define it's role in your thinking more clearly.

HENRY MILLER: First of all, I'm not really a Zen; if I were I wouldn't talk about it. What proves whether you are a true Zen is whether you talk about it or not. But Zen certainly attracts me. I am more and more convinced that I was born for it; that's why I love it so, and understand it so well. Do I live according to Zen principles now? I couldn't say. In fact no, I think not. I simply have my own conception of Zen, and am satisfied with that.

Others too have their own conception of Zen. You know, I live in California on the West Coast of the United States, and it's mainly in that part of the country that people are so drawn towards the East these days. It's odd because in the past, when Whitman and Emerson were alive, the East Coast was where people began to absorb Eastern ideas. Now it's mostly on the West Coast.

It makes me laugh to see all kinds of cults, sects and 'isms' cropping up at home in California . . . it's crazy. But it's not really so much a sign of this great confusion in America that everyone's always talking about. No, it seems to me that this confusion exists throughout the Western World. Anyhow, I think it's a good thing. It's more the sign of a period of transition. It's a good thing to be searching for something, don't you think?

GEORGES BELMONT: Taking up your art of living once again, there's one word I'd like to bring back into the conversation: the word I've already brought up as being essential in your work and yourself – the word 'heart'.

Among the titles of your books, there is one which I find especially revealing in this connection, *The Wisdom of the Heart*. Over here we are only familiar with fragments of this book, that appeared together with other fragments under a different title belonging to yet another work, *Sunday after the War*. I think we should clarify what you mean by 'the wisdom of the heart'.

HENRY MILLER: First of all I should explain how I came to use the word.

One day in London – no, even before that, in Paris . . . one day I was given a book by an English psychoanalyst, whose name I have since forgotten. He was a prominent psychoanalyst in Harley Street, and I was strongly influenced by his thinking. He had been to India and had become imbued with a great many aspects of Indian philosophy. In his book he devoted a lot of space to this word 'heart'. As far as I can remember the book was called *War Dance*, but despite the title there was a great deal in it about the 'heart'. Also, the other evening I was rereading what André Gide wrote about Dostoyevsky and was struck by the realization that Dostoyevsky too always distrusted the intellect. He even tells us it's the devil himself – the great temptation into which the devil tries to lead us. Dostoyevsky's heroes, his main characters like Prince Mishkin, are all people who put feeling above intellection. Yes, intellection is the great temptation.

I finally met this English psychoanalyst later on, in London. To my great surprise there was nothing of the psychoanalyst about him; he was more like a Hindu sage. He was at the same time totally English, but very much imbued with Hindu thought. He too was intending to prove that feeling should predominate over all – heart, and not the mind, not intelligence. That's all I can say. For the moment, that's all I know. But when I read the wise men of the East, I seem to meet with the same thing again. They are forever repeating that the heart is the important thing.

GEORGES BELMONT: Within the heart there are also the *impulses* of the heart, generally known as the passions. Are these passions part of the wisdom of the heart?

HENRY MILLER: They certainly are! William Blake has said so: 'The tigers of wrath are wiser than the horses of instruction'. That's another way of expressing what I was saying.

If you follow the dictates of the heart, the result may be conflicting passions, but it doesn't much matter; it's much more worthwhile than living out one's life *there*.

GEORGES BELMONT: *There*, meaning in your head?

HENRY MILLER: Reason, logic and the rest.

GEORGES BELMONT: In other words the vagaries of the passions seem to you to be part of the wisdom of the heart as well?

HENRY MILLER: No, because when one has attained wisdom, the conflict is, in principle, done away with.

GEORGES BELMONT: Do you feel that you've got to the stage of overcoming most of your conflicts?

HENRY MILLER: Oh, no! I hope I shall never reach that point. I'd like to stay . . . how shall I say? . . . I don't like perfection. I want to stay perpetually in conflict with myself. I find that extremely sound and healthy. You get something out of it. If there's one prayer I still say to God, it's this: 'Preserve me from ever being a sage!'

I love serenity. When I see Buddha with his incommensurable smile, it's marvellous. But I know that I shall never reach that stage, and have no desire to. I should like above all, and as far as possible, to be a man like any other. I like making mistakes, and enduring defeats too. Something results – an additional richness. That's what wisdom is, this process of continual enrichment; to enter into the fullness of life.

Nirvana is not at all what people think it is, a state of blissful contemplation. No, it's something gained, an achievement. And things are not achieved without struggle. It's pure idiocy to think that one can reach perfection and then there'll be no more conflict! That would be a living death.

GEORGES BELMONT: And yet just now you said that conflict abates, and even disappears with age?

HENRY MILLER: Oh, that's just a way of putting it! Whenever I look at myself in the mirror I still see a man in torment. I'd really like to be able to talk like a sage, I'd like to be a sage, but I know I'll achieve neither, and at bottom I'm happy enough to be as I am and stay that way.

It's strange, don't you think, that Heaven shouldn't be

popular? People are always choosing Hell. Hell is so much more interesting!

GEORGES BELMONT: Do you think you've often chosen Hell, in your life?

HENRY MILLER: Oh yes! Perhaps not deliberately, strictly speaking, but unconsciously, yes. I have always been more attracted to Hell than Heaven.

GEORGES BELMONT: Could it be that Hell seems to you the natural path to wisdom?

HENRY MILLER: Yes. I'll quote William Blake again: 'It's through Hell that one reaches Heaven'. You must descend before you ascend. To me that's indisputably true.

GEORGES BELMONT: Do you consider Hell, conflict that is, as being more profitable and productive, from the creative point of view?

HENRY MILLER: Yes, certainly. There's absolutely no doubt about it.

GEORGES BELMONT: More profitable and productive than Heaven?

HENRY MILLER: Without the slightest doubt. That's why I always prefer to depict the bad side of things and people. It's infinitely more exciting and *alive*.

I can't even imagine life in Heaven. My secretary, Gerald Robitaille, has written a play in which God comes down to earth to take a look at what's going on. He's been out of touch with everything for centuries . . . dozing. All of a sudden he gets interested in the world, and decides finally to go and take a trip to Hell to see what that's like. And there he's got good company. He finds Rabelais, the Marquis de Sade, Gilles de Rais, and all kinds of 'monsters', as they say. He acknowledges and proclaims that they are the best of company, and that there are no more interesting fellows.

In a way that reminds me of what D. H. Lawrence wrote about Jesus . . . you know, that book of his where Christ is back on earth after the resurrection. But this time Christ is a totally normal man, a man like any other you might say, almost a fool. But, there is one difference: he finds life wonderful now . . . yes he *enjoys life*, do you see? Simply because he has shed his personality, and with it his morbid fears, and his mania for wanting to save the world. These are things one must rid oneself of. To want to save the world is more than a vast mistake, it's a boundless transgression.

GEORGES BELMONT: Do you consider that the world is capable of saving itself?

HENRY MILLER: It's a question I very often ask myself. I can manage to conceive of it, but always with the thought in mind that there would have to be a massive catastrophe of some sort, something completely unforeseen. Then, under the impact of this terrible occurrence, man would at that moment perhaps attain another level of consciousness. Everything he was would fall away from him. The problems confronting us today would not be resolved, but would be forgotten. Their whole fundament would be swept away, or rather they would collapse utterly, of their own accord. But don't you think it's a little foolish to talk of such things?

GEORGES BELMONT: Why?

HENRY MILLER: Because we're talking about impossibilities rather than possibilities, aren't we? Mind you, I often tell myself, 'Better the impossible than the probable. The impossible is a thousand times more interesting!'

And then again, deep down, I am convinced that nothing is impossible . . . I repeat nothing, because I also believe that, however long mankind's history may be, he has, throughout the ages, been a long way from ever beginning to live like a man. It was Lawrence again who said: 'A dog is always a dog, a horse a horse, a flower a flower: but is a man always a man? He's not a man yet'.

In fact, man has not yet understood what is within him, and what he potentially represents. He'd need to undergo a tremendous shock in order to truly become a man . . . to transcend his present condition . . . his condition for centuries past. Believe as I may what I said about psychoanalysts, that doesn't prevent man's really drastic need for psychoanalysis!

▢▢▢▢

GEORGES BELMONT: You had a very hard start in life. Did the difficulties and insurmountable barriers you came up against, in your early manhood and years as an artist, act as a kind of filter, a catharsis? Did they cause things to fall away from you, to use your own words?

HENRY MILLER: Oh, no doubt about it.

You know, it's always difficult to say where one is at. Really all I can say is that in the midst of my conflicts I am at peace with myself, and I don't think that's so bad, do you? I ask for nothing more. And more than that, the creative man in me is, in my view, less important than the man who can live at peace with himself. I believe that I could give up the creative side – repudiate it, almost – if I could be sure of finding complete peace with myself.

And anyway, creative men! . . . this taste we have for genius! . . . Don't you in fact agree? There are very few creative artists, and we make gods of them, almost. There's nothing worse. It would be a much better thing to destroy not only the cult but also the creations of great men . . . to have no more great men in the accepted sense. Yes, it would be infinitely better for everyone to be creative on his own level . . . the degree of creation of which he is capable. Infinitely better that we should be each of us creators in our own separate ways, instead of worshipping our great men, as we call them. It's too facile to be content just to worship. It's idleness . . .

Forgive me, but something has suddenly struck me : these questions you're asking me, I wonder whom you're really asking – the man I was, or the man I am today? Because I think that when you've created something, and once it's finished, then you have done with it, and at the same time with what you were *before*. *After*, you develop and you're no longer the same man. At least I hope that's the case with myself – or will be. I've no desire to become a kind of duplicating machine, nor to be a man who's always struggling. Even if one never ceases to struggle, the fight goes on at different levels. That's what I should like : to struggle, but to continually change level.

It's true to say that the questions I'm generally asked seem to be directed at the man who created the *Tropics*, the man who made another life for himself. But no one ever wonders whether I'm still that man, nor even whether I'm still the man I was in that other life . . . and what other life that was?

GEORGES BELMONT : Perhaps it's that you're such a complete man – that you are so completely yourself in every way, I mean – that what you call development is, in your case a kind of growth or, more precisely, the fact that you broaden out concentrically as a tree does?

You retain everything. First and foremost you are a man who remembers. So much so that you felt the need to write a book with the title *Remember to Remember* (*Souviens-toi de te Souvenir,* and not *Souvenirs Souvenirs* as it was translated). And in spite of the fact that your memory becomes enriched by these other selves, it is the *same* memory, and this memory, always integrally yours, has become your opus . . . an opus which, indeed, is always opening outwards, whilst being entirely closed in on itself – closed in, I mean, like a constantly expanding universe.

HENRY MILLER: That's a great compliment you're paying me.

GEORGES BELMONT: I would not, were it not the truth. To come back once more to this word which seems to me to express the essence of yourself and your work : at the centre, there's the heart, and around it the man and his memory develop – it's the heart which dictates action, and which safeguards identity. With this in mind and since, in your own words, the struggle continues but on other levels, what stage is it at now?

HENRY MILLER: Wait, let me think . . .

At the present state of things, there are two things I'd like to overcome – to acquire, more exactly . . .

It's strange, but one of these things is patience. Most people imagine me to be a very patient man, whereas I myself am convinced of the opposite. The very moment I want something, I have to have it right away. And nothing ever satisfies me. Everything always comes too late . . . too late for me. I get eaten up inside : I say to myself, 'When's it going to happen? When? When? Tomorrow? Tomorrow? . . .' whereas in reality I have to reckon on a year, perhaps two, before getting what I want.

It's not always my fault, mind you. I find that despite

all this progress that people are always talking about, man and the world are terribly ineffective; we are always behindhand.

I should like to have miracles the whole time. Even if God gave me everything I want now, I'd demand more and still more, and fast, very fast! . . . It's one of the contradictions in me.

GEORGES BELMONT: Are you quite sure that this is a contradiction? Doesn't it form part of the creative force within you which finds it quite natural that things should come to it quickly, because it does not wait to reveal itself? And since, with you, life is closely bound up with creation, isn't it to be expected that you should be quite as impatient in life as well?

HENRY MILLER: That's very possible.

When I think about it, what strikes me in the story of Jesus, and what I like about him above all is that when he gets himself involved in performing a miracle, it happens right away. The sick man is cured at once. And to me that's truth, absolute truth; everything should happen like that.

I don't believe in evolution, I believe in miraculous things which don't happen step by step, but all at once, suddenly. And that should be not only absolute truth, but the most normal thing in the world.

GEORGES BELMONT: You mean that it seems normal to

you that the apparently least normal of occurences should come about, and happen in the most normal of ways?

HENRY MILLER: Exactly. The only trouble is that, in life as we live it, the opposite is the norm . . .

Oh, the world, the world! . . . In one's most perfect moments of reflection one comes finally to the conclusion that the world cannot be other than it is – with all its evils, all its wickedness and imperfections. But all that matters little in the final analysis, the moment one becomes one's true self . . .

Some people tell you that even as it is, the world is good, and life is a beautiful thing. Personally I don't go that far. Still, some days you feel good; you get up in the morning, you see that the problems are still there, just like they were the day before and the day before that, like good sentries at their posts; you pick up the paper, open it – as usual, nothing but disasters, wars, revolutions – and yet you still go on feeling good, all these everyday clouds clear away. You say to yourself, 'What's all that got to do with me? I am happy, today I am content, life is wonderful . . .' I find that this is a very sound attitude. You could call it a logical way of looking at things. The trouble is where does logic lead, and to what?

GEORGES BELMONT: And the days when you feel bad?

HENRY MILLER: Yes, those days everything is bad, and goes badly.

GEORGES BELMONT: Even if all's right with the world?

HENRY MILLER: Even if all's right with the world, yes.

GEORGES BELMONT: Do you feel that there have been many miracles in your life?

HENRY MILLER: Yes, it has been continuously filled with miracles . . . miracles with a small 'm'. Full of miraculous events, yes.

Many times I've been near to death, physically and spiritually, and each time I've been saved at the last moment. By whom? By what? At these righteous moments I look up at Heaven and say, 'Thanks, I know you're there, thanks a lot . . .' I don't mean that there's an actual person, but there is always 'someone', a power, call it what you like, which saves me. I am protected. I have a strong sense of being protected in this way. And consequently I say, 'For myself, I do nothing; it is *done* for me.' Despite all my lapses and all my mistakes, I regularly *get* saved. Why? I haven't the slightest idea. It's my destiny. And besides, everyone has his own individual destiny.

For myself, I believe in destiny. I believe in it absolutely because I have seen men who have lived surrounded by the terrors and horrors of life – in prison, in wartime, during persecutions – and they would come through everything unscathed. And knowing as I do the life they've lead, the difficulties and the grief they've known and overcome, and the way they've come out of it, I can positively say that these experiences have only served to enrich them. You've got to admit, haven't you, that misfortune contributes to people's enrichment.

GEORGES BELMONT: Don't you think that this saving force is to some extent yourself?

HENRY MILLER: Ah, that I don't know. I don't even ask myself that question. I see my mistakes clearly, and how I commit them, but I fail totally to understand the workings of my own deliverance. Often, when it happens, I'm at the end of my tether, totally incapable of doing anything. And just at that moment I get a sort of moment of illumination. Everything is . . . how shall I put it? . . . lifted from my shoulders, all at once, *just like that!* That's when I think that I am nothing, I can do nothing. Yes, at that very instant when the Protector, or whatever, suddenly gets me out of it all.

I frequently say – and the French don't like this much, and the Germans still less – 'It's when you renounce, when you surrender, that miracles happen. The whole thing is knowing how to surrender. But that's what is necessary'.

GEORGES BELMONT: It is in fact a gift you possess and your work demonstrates the fact as much as your life. And with you that seems to go hand in hand with another gift: to be able to, and to know how to give. You give a great deal. You take a great deal too. But above all, you give. And I wonder whether it's not the combination of these two essential virtues – to know how to renounce and how to give – which finally constitutes this strength, this power that always proves to be your salvation.

HENRY MILLER: You know, I like my answers to be thought of in terms of mystery. I love mystery. I believe that life is nothing but mystery . . . a mystery we shall never penetrate. That's why I don't much like what scientists and politicians get up to. I find them both equally futile.

GEORGES BELMONT: Futile?

HENRY MILLER: Yes, to do what they do. I am convinced that no matter what period or century I lived in, past or future, I would still think the same way as I do today. My happiness is not dependent, so to speak, on inventions, innovations or progress. They are quite irrelevant.

I sense that you are going to speak to me of contradictions, because these days I demand all modern comforts. The fact is I'm becoming weak, physically, I mean. I can no longer grow old without comforts. I should like to do without them, but I no longer can.

GEORGES BELMONT: But you don't worship your comforts. For you they are still *creature* comforts?

HENRY MILLER: Yes, I hope only that. At my place I have my water-colours hung all over the walls – I even paint on the walls themselves sometimes – but I haven't much furniture. I have no aesthetic sense where interior decoration is concerned. All I want to be certain of is having a room where I can play ping-pong, just one room, how it looks doesn't matter. In my house in California it's the best room in the place. Before, it was the lounge but I said to myself, 'The hell with the lounge! I don't give a damn, I'll have it for ping-pong . . .'

Some years before all that, I was there entirely alone for two or three months on end. My wife, the mother of my two children, had walked out and everything in the house, the furniture, even the carpets, belonged to her. She took the lot, and overnight I was left with an empty house, a completely empty house. On top of that the rooms were all pretty big, and all the floors were bare. So I decided to go and buy some roller-skates. I'd trundle from one room to the other. It was marvellous, too, to have no more possessions. I was a hundred times happier in that emptiness than I had been surrounded by furniture. What little furniture I subsequently bought was worth nothing, and was very cheap. It was all the same to me.

Look, even these days, I've a friend who brings me a present every time he comes to see me – almost always a piece of furniture, a chair, anything. He's convinced that I need some, and each time I tell him, 'No, no, take your present back where it came from! I've quite enough stuff as it is!'

And it's true. I don't like being hemmed in. Basically, I think I quite like austerity. And anyway, as I say, I don't give a damn for aesthetics. I very much like the Japanese aesthetic sense; it's possibly the thing I admire most about them. But that doesn't prevent me from personally not giving a damn for it.

I was talking a moment ago about the walls of my present home in California . . . Well, in the room where I do my water-colours the walls are covered with words, names, quotations from my favourite authors, and also drawings, and I let everyone do exactly what he wants on these walls. It's a kind of desecration, I know, but that's a term I'm very fond of. I tell people who come to see me, 'This is my house. I'm free to do anything I want. Do the same!' As a result there are graffiti in all languages – Chinese, Japanese, German, Russian. When I look at these graffiti most of the time I don't understand a word, but it's amusing, and above all it's good to look at. I never get tired of them.

Even I sometimes suddenly get up in the middle of the night because I've just read something remarkable, and write it on the wall. Other times I'll write about moments in my life . . . transcribing them, so to speak, into idiotic or obscene language . . . anything!

Not long ago, for example, I went through a phase like that. I had insomnia. I'd get up at three in the morning and begin a water-colour, but at the same time as painting I would write, mixing up the words and the colours. It was no good me telling myself, 'It's stupid, it's a mess, it's crazy, utterly crazy!' I couldn't stop myself from going on. In one sense I was ruining the water-colour, but all the same something came out of it . . . a mix-up, granted. Think of the illustrations in old manuscripts, of Persian or other painting. Calligraphy played a large part. The trouble is that in our Western languages calligraphy no longer exists, as it still does in China and Japan. But I afford myself the luxury of imitating Japanese or Chinese on my walls, or in my water-colours. And the oddest thing is that sometimes I have Japanese or Chinese visitors who look at what I've written and exclaim, 'But those signs mean such-and-such in my language!' And to think that I drew out those signs instinctively fills me with joy . . . now that really is comfort for you! . . .

Regarding this word 'comfort', I've just remembered an expression. Jesus is referred to as the 'great comforter' . . . In French, you say *'grand consolateur'*. But *'grand réconforteur'* would be so much better.

'Réconforter' is a very good verb, a great word. It's comforting we need, not comfort. The important thing is that someone should listen to you when you're in a fix. Someone who hasn't got whatever you want, either to say, or to give – someone who is just happy to listen. Knowing how to listen is a great thing, wouldn't you say?

GEORGES BELMONT: Yes, that's another of your gifts.

I remember that before the war we often used to sit together in front of a café, and someone would come along – a man obviously 'in a fix' as you just said, or sometimes a tramp, and all of a sudden he'd stop in front of our table. I remember two cases in particular: once on the terrasse of the Dôme, on the Boulevard Montparnasse, and another time on the terrasse of a little café on the right as you go up the Rue Vavin. And those weren't the only times . . . Yes, suddenly a man would stop, someone who was a complete stranger to both of us (you weren't famous at the time), and this stranger would speak to you, or rant at you. The one on the Rue Vavin insulted you, I remember. But, it should be stressed, they were never drunks. On each occasion, after a little while, you'd invite them to sit down at our table. And on each occasion the man would gradually begin to pour out his whole life and all his problems to you. It would last sometimes an hour or two. You'd say nothing, you'd hear him out, just nodding and humming to yourself the way you sometimes do, a deep humming sound which is a complex sign with you – reflection in progress, patient or impatient attentiveness, but also escape from your surroundings. . . . You'd hear him out and then, when he ran out of steam, you'd pass judgement. It could be a firm verdict, or advice.

HENRY MILLER: Advice? Oh, that *is* bad!

GEORGES BELMONT: It all depends on the kind of advice.

I remember you told that man on the Rue Vavin that the best and simplest thing to do was to go and jump in the Seine. And you were right; it was certainly the best way of bringing him face to face with himself.

HENRY MILLER: At all events there was no malice on my side.

GEORGES BELMONT: No, none at all. It did him good. He thanked you. I am sure that he didn't jump in the Seine and probably, for a few hours at least, he was in good spirits.

I am sure too that in such cases what people sense in you is precisely the comforting presence of someone acutely conscious of life. I have always had the impression as I watch you live your life that your salvation, that great saving strength of yours which allows you to come out of everything unscathed, is still this tremendous confidence you have, not only in yourself, but in life itself.

HENRY MILLER: Yes. I have always insisted that life is good, even when it is bad; that men are failures, washouts, but that life is good.

Once again we're getting back to that broad discrimination which characterizes Chinese philosophy; there's only one life and it is always good . . . more than good, much more. It is man who is mad, and unequal to the situation.

One does not have the right to speak of good or evil when talking about life. Life is energy – tremendous energy. What do morals and ethics have to do with it? Isn't it almost a question of health, of well-being? Vital energy, that's what life is. I have no hesitation in saying that, even if it gives the 'intellectuals' a laugh. Man has set up religions, ethical systems and moral values that contravene life, go against it's meaning, against what I call well-being.

Actual good-health is just the opposite.

GEORGES BELMONT: Does that, for instance, mean that the wisdom of the heart cannot exist without the whole person being generally healthy?

HENRY MILLER: That's it. And in exactly this connection I remember a book containing diagrams depicting some mechanical contraption, a system of pipes, of which the philosophy, so to speak, was this: that the water must keep flowing all the time, that blood must keep flowing and circulating, that there should be no blockages anywhere, that everything should keep on flowing. It comes, and passes on its way. To be healthy is to keep a living current flowing.

□□□□

GEORGES BELMONT: Just now you were talking about fate and your faith in it. There was a time before the war when you were very interested in astrology, and also believed very much in it.

HENRY MILLER: Yes, and I still do. You are alluding to the relationship between fate and astrology and the problem of choice, I suppose? These are indeed fundamental questions. Since the dawn of creation the debate has been open: choice, free will, or the opposite, determination and determinism? As far as I am concerned there is one distinction above all which interests me. In English the word for '*destin*' is fate . . . what's that in French?

GEORGES BELMONT: '*Sort*'. It's the Latin *fatum*.

HENRY MILLER: '*Sort*', yes that's it. I should like to know: in your view is there a difference between '*destin*' and '*sort*' or could it not be, let us say, a strong nuance?

GEORGES BELMONT: To me, '*sort*' is chance, to a much greater degree; '*destin*' indicates guided chance.

HENRY MILLER: Yes.

GEORGES BELMONT: Guided by a higher, external force . . .

HENRY MILLER: That's it, yes.

GEORGES BELMONT: In no way by man. When man intervenes, you have destiny; a force both composite, and one that actively compounds . . . that results from the action of the will, and a degree of free will, upon fate and destiny.

HENRY MILLER: Yes, I believe that fate intervenes only when man is not following his destiny, when he's not conscious of it, when he does not *know* what his destiny is — which comes down to what is surely your idea of predestination. And so he falls to his death. Isn't that what is called fatality?

When a man doesn't fulfil his destiny, fate drags him along by the tail. Not a bad image, eh?

GEORGES BELMONT: Excellent, but one that is hardly in keeping with yourself.

Just now, when we were talking about the art of living, I had in mind a story you told me some years ago . . . about this Hindu sage, a swami whom you'd gone to see one day . . .

HENRY MILLER: Ah, yes. It happened at a time when I was pretty shaken up and had troubles. It must have been about twenty-five years ago. It was in Hollywood. I was in love with a Greek girl – very much in love. Not counting other problems. In short, as I remember, I was on the brink of suicide. And someone said to me : 'Why don't you go and consult this *swami*?' In actual fact I'd already heard of him, but didn't know him personally – only by name and reputation. All I knew was that he was called Provavananda, and was a friend of Aldous Huxley.

In the end I phoned him, and asked : 'Could you give me an appointment, just so that we can have a few words? Just a few minutes?' . . . And he at once replied, 'But of course. Come whenever you want.' I said, 'Tomorrow?', and he said, 'Tomorrow, fine.'

Well, this is what's odd : that very evening, yes, during the night following the day I'd phoned him and consequently before the appointment, all my problems were solved, all my confusion had been dispersed, had flown away! Completely! Miraculously! . . . although 'miraculously' is not the right word, no. Rather, it had to do with the way he'd said to me right away, 'But of course, come. I am at your disposal, at your service. *Come whenever you want.*' I believe that that was the cure.

Even so the next day I kept the appointment. I remember it well. I knocked, he opened the door, and I said to him, 'Good morning. Forgive me, but, I've no more need of you. Everything is solved, all my problems have disappeared'. And he took me by the hand and said, 'Come

in anyway. Perhaps it is I who need you. I too have problems. Perhaps you can help me . . .' It was marvellous!
And I went in and spent an hour with him; we talked. Perhaps I really did help him, in any case he was keen to give
me that impression. Only a great man can do that, and
say the things he did. In a sense, he was the miracle. Yes,
the miracle was without doubt his immediate consent to see
me, when I asked for an appointment.

What we need, in that sort of situation, is a sympathetic
ear, someone who is prepared to listen, and to do so im-
partially, without being indulgent or compromising. You
know very well what happens when a friend is in a jam
and he happens to phone up to tell you about his problems.
You listen to him, but at the same time you're thinking:
'Oh, dear me, what's up with him now? What's all the
fuss about?' The truth of the matter is that in those cases
our reaction is tainted most of the time, and if it's tainted
it's because we ourselves are tainted.

GEORGES BELMONT: It was however out of a form of
purity on your part that you kept the appointment with
the swami, when you were already rid of your problems?

HENRY MILLER: Perhaps so ... unless it was the con-
ventional side of me. Or again, out of curiosity.

Basically I had great respect for this man, after what I'd
been told about him, and the idea of being able to speak
so easily and openly with a swami was surprising enough
in itself.

GEORGES BELMONT: And in the end you in turn helped him? I'm sure he didn't tell you that just to give you pleasure.

HENRY MILLER: I don't know. But I listened to him and we became friends. Yet the strange thing is that we never followed up our relationship. The reason? I've no idea. In the same way, when an exceptional moment of empathy occurs between someone and myself, I often cut off the relationship; I wouldn't want another, slighter moment between us, do you see?

This swami and I had no more need of each other; it was a thing of the past, the first meeting was enough.

GEORGES BELMONT: Is that an attitude which, once again, derives from your wisdom of the heart?

HENRY MILLER: It's possible. At several junctures in my life I've met men of the same temper as this swami, but without seeing them again, or never more than once. After that, finish.

But these men dwell on in my memory, and their influence is often greater than that of people with whom I have lived all my life, whom I know well, and who are friends. They enter into my life for a moment, and what they've done for me in that moment is incalculable. All, without exception, in the space of that short time, have proved to me that they knew me better than certain life-long friends. Yes, that's a curious and not particularly comforting thing, don't you think?

GEORGES BELMONT: Why so?

HENRY MILLER: Oh, well now . . . it's not so funny to think that old friends may know you less well than a stranger, someone you see for just a short moment in your life.

GEORGES BELMONT: Perhaps your friends have a fixed idea of you, and to a large degree they think of you in terms of that idea?

HENRY MILLER: Yes, perhaps.

GEORGES BELMONT: I should think that the men who afforded you these extraordinary encounters have never been what one would call great men in the usual sense?

HENRY MILLER: No, generally speaking, not.
The swami was an exception. He was a great man. There have been other swamis in my life. Several, even. There was one in New York, with whom I felt perfectly at ease, but in another way . . . in no way impressed at all. He wasn't much respected. But I used to respect him because I'm made that way, but not at all as a disciple respects a master. To me he was a worldly man, and I was a bit wary of him. He knew how to keep his head above water; he certainly didn't have any problems . . .
You know, there's much to be said on this disciple–master relationship business. The best thing is to speak in parables . . . The disciple sends word to the sage, who lives in a re-

mote part of the forest, asking whether he can come and see him. And the sage sends his reply, 'Of course . . . come and see me.' Only, you see, it is a very long way. However, the disciple sets off. There are obstacles at every step, and of course it is the master who has set them up. But if the disciple reaches the end, if he overcomes all the obstacles and succeeds in reaching the master, then the two of them meet as equals, as peers. In a word, what counts is not the master, but the path.

GEORGES BELMONT: I recall something very fine you said to me two years ago when you came to Paris for the exhibition of your gouaches.

We were looking at some photographs which were also on exhibition in the gallery and, you remember, among them there was a really extraordinary full-face portrait of a Chinaman. I asked you who he was and you replied, 'No one. I don't know the man.' Then you added, 'And yet for me, he's almost a master.'

HENRY MILLER: Yes, that's so. In one way, he's even my only master. For I have no masters in my life, and recognize none. In a way, it's a pity. If there's one thing I regret, it's never having found a man to whom I could say, 'Master'. Moreover, that goes for the whole Western World; it has no masters any more than I do. I have always hoped, and still do hope, to meet one – a true Zen master, for instance. But I always tell myself that if this meeting should come about, it would probably be somewhere unexpected : in the street, a bar, a whorehouse . . . And it would be easy, because he would be exactly like me. As I was saying a moment ago, we would be equals; there would be no question of a master–disciple relationship between us.

The Chinaman on my wall you talk about . . . well, until the day I die he will stay a complete unknown. I found his photo in a magazine about thirty years ago; I cut it out and framed it because when I looked at the eyes, the expression struck me so forcibly that I said to myself, 'Here is my master.' Yes, right away I thought that I should like to be like him and to have, above all, that look that he had.

It's hard to define that look. Detached, but not in the least indifferent; removed from turmoil, you might say. And the smile . . . in no way mocking but full of humanity . . . as though this man were embracing you with his smile. And then again, I have to admit, there is a strange resemblance between this unknown Chinaman, doubtless photographed by chance in some street, and my grandfather who was German and had nothing Chinese about him. But I don't think that was a determining factor in the attraction I felt as soon as I saw that face.

You know, when I meet someone I don't know, there are two things I look at right away: firstly the eyes, and then the mouth. Having said that, in the case of women, curiously enough, it's the opposite way round: first the mouth, then the eyes.

GEORGES BELMONT: Why the eyes first, with men?

HENRY MILLER: Because I have a point of comparison. I don't think that there is a single sage, a single oriental

saint whose portrait I've seen, who hasn't perfect eyes . . .
I mean rounded like eggs, and luminous even if they are
stone-hard. You can't find a trace of rancour, envy or
jealousy in them. Everything about them is limpid . . . so
simple and clear that it's almost as though you were looking right through and there was nothing on the other side
to see. It's the kind of look which takes in the world, the
whole universe with utter equanimity. The look of men who
are not searching . . . Yes, it's the absence of curiosity
which strikes me most about their eyes. Not that they haven't
ever searched, but that they've finished with all that. They
have 'arrived', do you see?

GEORGES BELMONT: And the mouth?

HENRY MILLER: The mouth? Oh, I would like to see
only generous mouths. I don't like thin-lipped people. I
like full, sensual mouths . . . especially in women.

GEORGES BELMONT: That's why in their case you look
at the mouth first?

HENRY MILLER: Yes. And I'm not often wrong about
what it conveys.

GEORGES BELMONT: I'd like us to go back a little. We have spoken a lot about a certain religious feeling you possess and listening to you talk I was remembering the beginning of your book, *The World of Sex*, where you state with great precision the problem of this private world, and where you yourself declare 'It goes without saying that I am essentially a religious man, and always have been'. And then you go on to add: 'Some people will certainly wonder whether there isn't a conflict between sex and religion . . .'

Indeed it seems to me that that's a question many of your readers may ask themselves when confronted by your work?

HENRY MILLER: Yes, I can well understand that. However I'd like to make it clear right away that I don't know my books off by heart, and I can't remember what exactly I wrote in this particular one . . . I forget.

Having said that, it seems to me that there is no conflict between sex and religion. Absolutely not. Both are . . . how shall I put it? . . . necessary and innate. It is we who create the conflict with our cults. Particularly we Christians in the West. Speaking in very general terms, but none the less exact, it may be said that the West has contrived to fabricate a duality between body and spirit, whereas the East has striven to unite the two. For the East, there is no difference between body and spirit; they are indissolubly bound together. That is an idea, a way of looking at things, which seems to me very healthy and natural. I don't see what

ascetics with their austerity contribute. They are somehow
crippled and are, in my opinion, a very bad influence.

It's strange to think that the question of this duality
should always take on such importance in the framework
of our Western religions. In the East they think of it in the
simplest possible way. You've seen those great temples in
India, with their facades crammed with erotic figures which
exceed anything imaginable. Can one say that those temples
are the work of atheists or sensualists? No, they are the work
of deeply religious people. They represent a worship of the
flesh, of the body which leads men to the gods.

Naturally, I dislike being asked questions about sex, as
though I were an authority on the subject. I don't understand why I am considered to be one. To tell you the truth
I've gotten to the point where when someone utters the
word 'sex' in my presence I long to grab a gun and defend
myself, and yell, 'Death to sex!' Not that I really desire its
death, but to put an end to that sort of discussion about it.
Yes, I'm sick of them! I'm really sick of the fact that it's
the first and last question I'm ever asked. I'm no Freud or
Jung.

And then again, I've the impression that I've lived a very
normal life. And the only difference that exists between
others and myself is that I've said outright what they dis-
simulate behind a lot of words when they write their books.
But everyone behaves like me, and I behave like everyone
else. A sex life is the most natural thing in the world. I've
never tried to be a Don Juan, for instance. The idea never
occurred to me. The truth is that I even feel a bit shy with
women. It's always been they who have . . . let us say . . .

seduced me. I'm almost like an adolescent with them, like a kid.

GEORGES BELMONT: In fact, if I asked you that question, it is precisely because there is, I think, an ambiguous attitude to your name and work which it would be good to clear up.

You say for example, still in *The World of Sex*, that you can distinguish two distinct categories among your readers: those who find the sexual element in your work disgusting, and those who are delighted that it occupies such a large proportion of it. I think that you'd be more on the side of the delighted than the disgusted wouldn't you?

HENRY MILLER: Personally, yes, but basically that doesn't concern me. It's their business and not mine.

Naturally when you read a book, you interpret it according to your own nature, and also your own culture and ability to understand. But between ourselves, I don't give a solitary damn for my readers' problems. Once again, their reactions don't concern me, and if you ask my candid opinion, both categories are wrong.

GEORGES BELMONT: That's just what I wanted you to say.

HENRY MILLER: But it's true! When you read someone's work you mustn't choose the aspect of it that your nature or taste leads you to select. You've got to swallow the man whole, and raw . . . what you like and what you dislike.

GEORGES BELMONT: Exactly. I've always had the impression when reading your books, and sometimes when translating them, that what certain people call excessive sexuality on your part, and what your most acid critics even go so far as to call self-satisfaction in sexual matters . . .

HENRY MILLER: Self-satisfaction? But let me repeat, there is nothing more natural! Sex, sex . . . that's not the only thing in life!

GEORGES BELMONT: Exactly. That was what I was about to come to. The fact that you say it's not the only thing in life seems to me to stem from this deep understanding of human beings *in toto* which you possess, in the context of what we've been talking about.

HENRY MILLER: Let's concern ourselves with the century we live in. Are we in the twentieth century, or the fifteenth? I often wonder. Questions like that were valid in the fifteenth, in my opinion. But nowadays?

Aside from the present day, we have been leading very free sex lives in this Western world of ours for the last twenty years, haven't we? At our present stage, all questions on such matters seem to me to be idiotic. Be that as it may, people forget that in the classics, yes, in *all* the books by the great classic authors, they certainly don't pose the same problems about sex as they do today. It was accepted as something self-evident. Just think of Rabelais, Boccacio and all the rest, not to mention the Greeks and

Romans. And we're now in the twentieth century! No, all that is quite absurd, in my view.

Even in Middle Ages the co-existence of body and soul was accepted. Look at the cathedrals: to a certain extent their exteriors remind one of the Hindu temples I was talking about just now; they bear the mark of the human body, and this is most evident in the forceful expression of sexuality in the small sculptures on the cornices. Once you get inside, doubtless it's something else entirely. . . . You could think of man as a full-scale cathedral, in his way.

Yes, perhaps in a sense people were much freer in the Middle Ages, even taking into account the rigours and harshness of religious sentiment. They were freer in spirit, it seems to me.

And then you've got to admit all these questions, all this stuff about sex, is extremely hypocritical. The man who makes a show of being upset by these things in order to stir up his own indignation knows perfectly well that he leads the same life as I sometimes describe in my books. He doesn't want to admit it, that's all.

GEORGES BELMONT: And he won't allow that it should be spoken or written about either?

HENRY MILLER: Precisely. If people wonder what my attitude was when I wrote my books, I'll say either that I had no one attitude, or that my attitude was a perfectly natural one, that for me there has never been any difference whatsoever between sexual matters and the other things I talk about.

Yes, it's true you could say there's a lot of sex in *Sexus*. It's concentrated stuff. But that's with reference only to a certain period of my life. And yet because of this, people always seem to take me for some giant of pornography. That's wrong! And let no one come and tell me I'm abnormal. For myself, I think I'm perfectly normal . . . perhaps not normal enough!

I have not done as Rabelais did. He exaggerated, carried things to excess. That's something else entirely. When you exaggerate it's a way of excusing what you're doing – as though you wanted to grant yourself the right to be able to say, take it for what it is: satire, fantasy. And then people accept it's enormity . . . I mean enormous vulgarity, like you get in those Japanese drawings, the erotic ones, you know? Everything in them is exaggerated, but it's a sort of convention in the technique which you end up by accepting.

GEORGES BELMONT: By that do you mean that really what people are least willing to accept is the expression of normal sexuality?

HENRY MILLER: That's it, yes.

GEORGES BELMONT: But did you have a purpose in mind when you dealt with the normal expression of this side of human beings, with this side of life? Did you want to show that 'it' exists, and cannot be denied?

HENRY MILLER: Yes, certainly.

GEORGES BELMONT: . . . and if not, one is not a complete man, nor a complete woman? Is that the reason you have attributed this importance to sex in your work?

HENRY MILLER: Yes. And also, unconsciously perhaps, it was a liberation for me, a way of freeing myself from puritanism. Born in America as I was, and brought up by puritanical parents, it probably was a means of freeing myself, yes, I think so. *The World of Sex* I wrote expressly for the censor who was banning my books in the States . . .

GEORGES BELMONT: The same one with whom you were corresponding even before the war, and who used to tell you how he was sorry to have to censor you?

HENRY MILLER: Yes, him. And the oddest thing is that he became my staunchest champion. One day he said to me, 'Why don't you write an uninhibited book on this notorious subject? I'd like to know what your thoughts really are on it.' And that's how I wrote *The World of Sex*.

Only it musn't be forgotten that when you make an analysis of a given subject in a book, it's always something that comes *after* – something secondhand, in a sense. When I was writing my other books I didn't think at all as I did when I was writing that one, do you understand? An analysis, or what is called by that name, is never really an analysis. What you've got to do is jump feet first into experience, immerse yourself in it. That's where you find reality, truth; not in the analysis.

GEORGES BELMONT: You mean that analysis is necessarily always analysis of analysis and so on, and there's no end to it?

HENRY MILLER: Yes, there's no end to it.

GEORGES BELMONT: Very often, when reading certain passages in *Tropic of Cancer*, *Tropic of Capricorn*, and *Sexus* – to keep to those three – one gets the feeling that when you deal with the period of sexual excess in which you and others immersed yourselves at a certain time in your life, it seems that you were behaving and writing as a moralist, rather than a self-satisfied author?

HENRY MILLER: A moralist, me? You mean I spoke out 'against'?

GEORGES BELMONT: No, that's not it. I repeat that I am talking about a specific period of your life and not in general terms, and that I have the impression that you had at that time almost a feeling of revulsion, or let's say distaste at this excess.

HENRY MILLER: Disgust?

GEORGES BELMONT: When all's said and done, yes. But maybe I'm making this up?

HENRY MILLER: No, no. I'm thinking.

GEORGES BELMONT: I mean that this seems to me to be one of a number of things which, perhaps as a reaction, triggered off the explosion of your talent and your life?

HENRY MILLER: I'm not quite sure that I follow you there. Do you mean that I behaved in an exaggerated way?

GEORGES BELMONT: No, I mean that the exaggeration was in life itself.

HENRY MILLER: In life?

GEORGES BELMONT: Yes. Not in your work.

HENRY MILLER: An exaggerated sexuality, you mean?

GEORGES BELMONT: Yes, but in no way deliberate or of your own volition.

HENRY MILLER: Oh, but that seems simple enough!
When you aren't leading a good life, a rich, full life – full of culture, of all the good things – you lapse into sexuality. You see it happen with poor people – in India, for example, and in Egypt with the Arabs. It's more or less a general rule. Sexuality becomes the comforter, the great comforter. People want to fall away into nothingness.

GEORGES BELMONT: That's precisely what I meant by the word revulsion. Shall we say that in your case it was a sort of passive revulsion?

HENRY MILLER: Yes, I understand you better, now. That's why I wrote so vividly, exaggerated a lot, and blew everything up out of all proportion, inordinately so. But that's no reason for people nowadays to go ahead and say that I'm a 'giant of sex'. I was enthralled by the idea of sex, so to speak, the idea of sex in general.

GEORGES BELMONT: That's really why I have so often got that impression, especially when translating certain passages in *Capricorn* and *Sexus*, because when translating them one is obliged to go deeper into the work. As I say, I've had the impression that it was a means of getting away from sexuality.

HENRY MILLER: Yes, that's not impossible. Via a certain lack of moderation, exactly. . . . In a sense, it was another way of saying what I had to say.

Instead of talking about God, I talked about sex. Sex replaced God really, in a way. That may appear sacrilegious, but it shouldn't be taken that way. I think it's simply a case of substituting one for the other. For at that time I was still the same religious man. I have never lost this sense of religion.

GEORGES BELMONT: That seems quite evident to me having read certain other passages in your books. In contrast, one comes across sudden lyrical outbursts, shall we say to simplify things, great flights of idealism and idealisation of life, human beings and of love. You are a great idealist in matters of love, aren't you?

HENRY MILLER: Yes, true, true. Still, that doesn't stop me from being frequently criticized for not talking about love, for never showing myself to be someone who knows about love. Women especially criticize me for this. And I acknowledge the fact that in a way they're right, because I've made a mess of love in the true sense, real loves . . .

What can I say? I've already touched on this; I didn't want to talk about love with a capital 'L' in my books, and yet I had it within me, do you see?

GEORGES BELMONT: Isn't that what is called sexual modesty?

HENRY MILLER: Yes, I think that's the phrase.

GEORGES BELMONT: To return one last time to the character whose silhouette and white, almost chalk-white face are present in all your most turbulent books: is not Mona for you the very expression of . . .

HENRY MILLER: Of love? Yes.

GEORGES BELMONT: Of the love you have within you, as you were saying?

HENRY MILLER: Yes. And in every sense of the word. For sometimes she is the devil and God at the same time. She was, and is, the whole gamut of love.

GEORGES BELMONT: And she makes you yourself both devil and God?

HENRY MILLER: Yes. A good relationship, eh? The masochist and the sadist! What a marriage! Precisely the theme which is always coming into William Blake: the marriage of Heaven and Hell. And it's true to say that that depicts marriage in the most perfect sense of the term. A totally harmonious marriage is *not yet* a marriage in my view. There has to be this conflict, this torture between two people . . . But here I am speaking very subjectively, on a very personal level . . . It's a bit like what you get in Dostoyevsky. Yes, I find the same thing in his books.

I must say that if I think I understand men, the same doesn't go for women. Even now, I don't think I understand them. There are . . . depths in women which a man never plumbs. They're a totally different breed.

GEORGES BELMONT: Do you consider that it has to do with different mechanisms?

HENRY MILLER: Mechanisms?

GEORGES BELMONT: In man and woman, yes. Two different mechanisms as regards, let's say, feeling and reactions?

HENRY MILLER: Mechanisms? I don't understand.

GEORGES BELMONT: Two 'motive forces' then.

HENRY MILLER: Motive forces? No.

There's no substantial proof for what I mean; but for me a woman is always more of the earth . . . she is more of the earth and values the earth more than a man. Man belongs to the air. He's not firmly rooted in the earth. Do you understand me? Men have wings, and that's a great pity for them because we all belong to the earth, men and women alike.

I don't give a damn about the moon and the stars, any more than I do about philosophical ideas – and that's saying something because those are false. But I admire woman for being so much of the earth. And I have no hesitation in saying that what we men lack is the element of femininity. We must cultivate it in ourselves. As for women, they hardly have need of an element of masculinity. They are quite capable of getting by without it. Personally speaking, I want women to remain completely and uniquely women, whereas I would like men to be divided, at odds, hesitating between man and woman. I'd be hard put to it to explain why, though. . . !

GEORGES BELMONT: Let's look at the problem from another angle. Do you think, for example, that passion finds different expression in men and women?

HENRY MILLER: Yes, certainly. With women passion is always a very personal thing. But a man can feel passionately about abstract ideas, God, and so forth. Women have no need of that, it seems to me. Of the two, it is man who is fundamentally religious . . . another of his faults, if you ask me. That sort of aspiration is the undoing of men.

GEORGES BELMONT: Religious feeling, you mean?

HENRY MILLER: No not only that. That sort of aspiration in all spheres.

It's man who complicates life and makes living difficult, whereas for woman life is quite simple. I mean that as soon as a woman is loved and is well treated, she finds life rather easy to live. But man! . . . I've not yet discovered the man who is capable of living peacefully and simply. Yes, from the start man has lived a complicated life. Poor fellow!

GEORGES BELMONT: Does that mean in particular that in your opinion man comes closer to love with a capital 'L'? . . . that he is more readily capable of conceiving love with a capital 'L' than woman is?

HENRY MILLER: Absolutely. It's always being said that love is her whole life for a woman. And it's true. For her it's the most important thing of all. But she cannot know the love with a capital 'L' that man can know. She can sacrifice herself for *her* man, but not for the sake of love in the wide sense. For her that will always remain personal and restricted.

GEORGES BELMONT: Would you say that this perhaps explains the generally more possessive and exclusive quality of woman's love?

HENRY MILLER: Yes. It is a fact that she is generally more possessive than a man. But as for knowing why . . . I'm not sure I know the answer. I can only say that as far as I am concerned it's clear that she's made that way.

Ideas come from the man. He's the one who invents the categories, the complexities.

In reality a woman is perfectly capable of living like a man – that is to say, in her case, having several men. I would even say that it's not good for her to have just one man in her whole life. She is just as capable of handling her love affairs as a man is. It is man who has imposed on her the idea of staying faithful to one love.

Having said that, just try and imagine how a woman who stayed wholly womanly would manage to live! It's impossible for this reason: for centuries we have been living under a masculine hegemony.

We are told that in prehistoric times there was matriarchy, the domination of women. Well, for my part I'd be delighted to see that sort of rule return. Of course what I have in mind is not a matriarchy as practised by women in America; I don't like that sort of domination, it's bogus, it's war. I'm talking about the kind of rule when women, with their native wisdom would really run the world instead of men. With domination by men I see nothing but disasters. Man spends his time committing suicide and killing everything around him. He is a destroyer. Woman conserves.

GEORGES BELMONT: Don't you sometimes get the feeling that our Western society is evolving little by little towards a sort of return to matriarchy?

HENRY MILLER: Nowadays? No. I can see women imitating men, that's all; and it's just a caricature, not even plagiarism. Woman has no business aping man. She should behave like a woman, with her good sense which keeps her in contact with the earth, and eliminate all idyllic, sublime ideas of life. That's what her wisdom and simplicity ought to consist of.

GEORGES BELMONT: Don't you believe that in the case of woman, the possessive character of passion and love is bound up with the feeling of insecurity she feels in life generally, by virtue of the fact that man, in society as it is — is the principal provider and master of the house no matter what efforts woman makes to enfranchise herself?

HENRY MILLER: Yes, sure. But I'm waiting for the day when this society will disappear.

There is nothing more false than our way of life these days. Woman no longer has any chance whatsoever to display her femininity, nor to share life on an equal basis with man. And all this business about security and insecurity are solely the result of our spiritual insecurity. They have nothing to do with exterior conditions or circumstances.

GEORGES BELMONT: That connects with what you said at the beginning of these conversations: that all the feelings of insecurity that provoke conflicts between human beings come from the inner recesses of man himself, and are not the result of exterior causes. It is man who creates these causes.

HENRY MILLER: That is precisely my opinion. Only just try and say that these days! You've no right to say that! Sacrilege! Dangerous! And why? Because in our time people are convinced that all ills *already exist* in exterior conditions and surroundings, and derive from them. Personally I am convinced of the opposite.

Not that I am indifferent to security. I am the first to proclaim that it is a necessity for men to live like men and not animals. But man doesn't even live like an animal these days. I mean that he doesn't live as well as animals do. You can't say he actively *leads* a life. He is lead. He is in every respect on a lower plane than the animals, in my view.

What is most strange is that, at the same time, he is spiritual . . . he is capable of dreaming of God, of asking himself grandiose questions. But that doesn't prevent his life as an individual from being literally abominable. He lives like a rat, or even worse. When I say 'abominable', the term isn't strong enough, for he's become an abomination unto himself. He has become degraded – and to such an extent that, I repeat, I don't see that men have *yet* become men. At the very most robots, with no individuality, or hope . . . that's what's bad . . .

No, I must modify what I've just said . . . There are parts of the world where hope does exist, for human beings. And that's the great area of conflict today – between men for whom hope does exist and us who have lost it. When I say 'us' I mean above all we in the West. We have no great hope. We are somehow passive. Oh, there's no shortage of activity in the West; we exert ourselves a lot, but without . . . how shall I put it? . . . without warmth, without believing in our exertions, without hope. We do everything like machines – even when we make war!

GEORGES BELMONT: During one of our recent conversations, I reminded you of that famous English saying: East and West will never meet. Is that what you think?

HENRY MILLER: Oh no, not at all! On the contrary, I believe that they will meet. Besides, it has to happen, otherwise the catastrophe to end them all will come about.

And it is we in the West who should, who must make the effort because it is we who have spurned, rejected the East. People are always saying that the Chinese cannot and will not make a move, but the fault is ours; it is we who have humiliated the East. So it's up to us to make the gesture.

And that's leaving aside the fact that we have everything – or so much, anyway – to learn from the East. Whereas the East hasn't a great deal to learn from us unless you count – what? – gadgets, inventions, creature comforts? Right, fair enough, but what about the essential part of life, the life of the spirit and the soul? Soul, now then there's a word you don't hear any more. We no longer dare to utter it.

GEORGES BELMONT: Forgive me for going back once again to the past, but do you consider that this civilization which you have revolted against has since got into more serious straits?

HENRY MILLER: Oh, no doubt about it! I'm convinced that there is no hope for civilization as we imagine it.

Besides, it's always been a bogus word.

It doesn't even exist, this civilization. Do you think we can speak of civilized people when we are talking about men who spend their time killing each other? And if that were all! I'm not going to waste *my* time listing everything that goes against our idea of civilization.

In my lifetime I have met perhaps all in all ten individuals whom I'd go so far as to call civilized. Now, Marcel Duchamp . . . yes, for me, Marcel Duchamp was a civilized man. But even so, he wasn't on the level I'm thinking of. But he was so well adjusted to life, so tolerant, that I liked him very much.

No, to tell the truth, I can't see where they've got to, these civilized men of ours. I can see human beings always about to commit atrocities – that's what never ceases to astound me about present-day man. That a man should be able to think like a god, and be himself almost god-like – there's nothing astonishing in that – but how he can go ahead and let himself commit atrocities, I shall never understand.

I can believe that man is capable of raising himself to a higher level than he has reached in our day, that he is capable of becoming a superman, as they say, but I find hard to understand how he can be so much a devil.

GEORGES BELMONT: When you say 'superman' do you mean it in the Nietzschean sense?

HENRY MILLER: In the great sense, the beautiful sense.

GEORGES BELMONT: That of the heart?

HENRY MILLER: Yes. For example there can be no super-men in politics. Politics is fit for cretins.

But the man who serves humanity, who is a *server*, do you see? Not someone who is just a servant. Yes, someone who serves it, the man who has other men in mind, who actively wants to serve – that's your superman, in my view. Am I right, or not?

GEORGES BELMONT: Oh, quite right. But to get back to Nietzsche . . .

HENRY MILLER: The superman Nietzsche himself spoke of has always been misunderstood, misinterpreted.

What does Nietzsche say when he talks about war? That when there are two great powers who are radical enemies, or at least radically opposed to each other, like Russia and the United States today let's say, well, it's up to the stronger of the two to declare: 'We are invincible, we are the more powerful; so it is we who lay down our arms and surrender.' There's no other way to have done with wars, for good and all.

GEORGES BELMONT : Do you not have the feeling that there is present, in a certain philosophical outlook and attitude of mind which are progressively more prevalent among young people today, something of this way of looking at things, a tentative effort in that direction, even though they are muddled in their objective?

HENRY MILLER : In youth today? Oh, you know, I'm a bit sceptical of these young people.

Look, just now we were talking about sex. There has been an explosive reaction against puritanism, and the young are very caught up in that. But it's a reaction, and I think that it will pass, and that after a few years a balance will be found. Perhaps, who knows, it will even fall back in the opposite direction. It wouldn't be the first time in history. The wheel turns . . .

Certainly, even besides sex, people are undeniably claiming, searching for, and finding to some extent, a freedom which generally speaking has not been demanded nor sought for a long time, it seems to me. And it no longer has just to do with literature, the theatre and such like. It's in life itself.

The Marquis de Sade said, to put it briefly, that people have the right to do what they want with their bodies, that it is up to each individual to decide and no one else. But things are being taken further today. When you see these naked kids in the New York parks with their banjos, maybe you laugh at them, but at the same time it's very daring. And it's incredible to think that the police are there, the whole arsenal with them, and they just look on. Yes, when you think about it, you don't believe your eyes, you think that it's not possible; what is this world we're living in? And the flowers round their necks, the flowers in their hair, on their clothes – that's odd too, isn't it? It's even surrealistic, it really is!

But as for saying that because of all this these young people are bringing something *lasting* into our society – no! I doubt it very much. These are only trial runs, sorties as the Military say, skirmishes. I don't think it will last. Let's just say that I haven't enough confidence in man to be convinced that he'll make something lasting out of it.

Besides, the young are divided among themselves just as much as the adults. Some are very conservative, and they are not the ones with the most money. No, on the contrary the ones with more money are often the rebels.

I do see the trend taking shape, but I don't see the necessary fervour or discipline. In my opinion you've got to wait ten years or so in order to judge . . . when the kids who are twenty today are thirty, and are married, have children. I'd like to see what they say and how they'll act then.

It's easy to be a rebel at twenty, especially when it's all in order to abdicate, to renounce everything. Yes, very easy. But when there are mouths to feed, that's a different story! You know, lack of money is still the worst of evils. And since our society is nowhere near repudiating money . . .

GEORGES BELMONT: Apropos of rebels and revolution-
aries, that play you wrote comes to mind – *Just Wild about
Harry* – which constitutes your sole approach to the theatre,
and which I hope we'll manage to put on here one day.
Harry, the hero of the play, has been to war; he has come
back disgusted not only with all the killing and his fear of
it – a halfway cosmic fear – but also with a civilization that
could tolerate butchery and carnage. When he comes back
to civilian life, he opts for a life on the fringe of civilization,
he refuses everything, even to work; he becomes a pimp . . .

HENRY MILLER: More of a rogue.

GEORGES BELMONT: Doesn't he himself say: 'I'm a
good pimp, an honest pimp?'

HENRY MILLER: Ah, yes, but he's overstating things! –
or I am, I don't know . . . really, he doesn't make a voca-
tion out of it. He's capable of anything – everything bad, I
mean. But also, the way I look at it, of everything good.
He's capable of both, do you see? Of good and bad alike.
And because of that I like this character very much. It's
odd when I think of it, because really he has no qualities –
no impulses, no ambitions. He makes no progress at all; he
is stupid, ignorant, vain and boastful. He has nothing but
bad qualities, so to speak, and yet he has heart.

Basically, you see, when all's said and done, I really like the bums, the no-goods. I even adore them because I'm pretty . . . sick, yes, sick of *good* people, you see? *The good people, good consciences*, right? That kind of person does more harm than bad people – with the exception of Hitler. That is what I believe. Because, generally, those who are well-to-do and say they lead the good life, who say they care about other people are nothing but hypocrites, and they make me puke. I can't stand people like that. I prefer priests; they, at least, are real hypocrites. Yes, I prefer people who are two-faced and show it, because that's human, at any rate.

I like everything that's human. To be totally human is perhaps the nearest thing to being an angel. The idea of the angel is important to me. There are no angels, I know that. But all that is part of the array of symbols we use – God, angels, saints – and when you venture to use them these days people look at you and say: 'Oh, that's old stuff, it's archaic! In the twentieth century! . . .' And yet I'm still convinced that these words, these images – for they are images – find a correspondence with things that are deeply in us . . . a conception of purity. The realists are the ones who don't like all that.

GEORGES BELMONT: Rather like the words 'soul' and 'heart' that we've already talked about?

HENRY MILLER: Yes, it's the same thing.

GEORGES BELMONT: Isn't that the theme of one of your books, which I was re-reading recently, and which, moreover, you set somewhat apart from the rest of your work, *The Smile at the Foot of the Ladder?*

HENRY MILLER: The theme of the angel and the clown, you mean?

GEORGES BELMONT: Yes.

HENRY MILLER: That's true. And the most curious thing is that it should occur in the only book I didn't base on immediate experience, the only book of mine which is purely imaginary. It was commissioned, imposed on me, not in the sense of a commercial order, but because one day Fernand Léger asked me to write a book to go with some drawings he'd done. And I actually wrote it one line after the other, not knowing what would come next. But that symbol touches something very deep inside me . . . one of the depths I was talking about just now.

When I was young, after I had stopped studying, if anyone had asked me what I wanted to do in life, I would reply, 'To be a clown'. In passing, let it be said that this proves what I thought of myself at the time, eh? And yet, it was to mean something very genuine to me. Only then I had no inkling what a clown represents, or of the greatness and importance of his rôle. Later I discovered that unconsciously I still regard myself as a clown . . . I acknowledge myself a clown.

But I've also discovered that the clown and the angel are very close to each other.

□□□□

GEORGES BELMONT: There is one last question I'd like to put to you.

At one stage in these conversations, you spoke of the rôle which was assigned to each of us, which was, somehow, our personal destiny. Do you yourself have the impression that you have fulfilled your given rôle?

HENRY MILLER: Oh, I'm sure that's a question I wouldn't even ask myself! But I imagine that it must be the best rôle that could have been given me, since I have played it . . . right?

GEORGES BELMONT: There's really no other rôle you regret not having had?

HENRY MILLER: Another rôle? Yes, perhaps. But in another life, when another incarnation comes around. Then – I think I've often told you this – I'd like to be an ordinary man in my next life—a nobody, as we say in English – the opposite of a somebody . . . no one at all. Yes, if I ever return to this earth, I should like to be the humblest of men, an unknown, *who would be of no consequence.* That is my ideal.